THe
Power
OF A
Positive
Teen

About the Authors

Best-selling author Karol Ladd has teamed up with her daughters, Grace and Joy, to write a powerful book for teens. Karol's award-winning titles include *The Power of a Positive Mom, The Power of a Positive Wife,* and *The Power of a Positive Friend.* Her uplifting and encouraging message offers biblical truth and hope for women of any age. Now with her new title for teens she blends her positive points with her daughters' experience, wit, and perspective. Together, the three Ladd girls hope to make a positive impact on the next generation.

author of the best-selling Power of a Positive series

Karol Ladd
Grace and Joy Ladd

THe
Power
OF A
Positive
Teen

HOWARD BOOKS
A DIVISION OF SIMON & SCHUSTER
New York   London   Toronto   Sydney

Our purpose at Howard Books is to:

- *Increase faith* in the hearts of growing Christians
- *Inspire holiness* in the lives of believers
- *Instill hope* in the hearts of struggling people everywhere

Because He's coming again!

HOWARD
BOOKS

Published by Howard Books, a division of Simon & Schuster, Inc.
1230 Avenue of the Americas, New York, NY 10020
www.howardpublishing.com

The Power of a Positive Teen © 2005 by Karol, Grace, and Joy Ladd

Library of Congress Cataloging-in-Publication Data
Ladd, Karol.
    The power of a positive teen / Karol Ladd, Grace and Joy Ladd.
        p. cm.
    Includes bibliographical references.
    10 Digit ISBN: 1-58229-435-6; 13 Digit ISBN: 978-1-58229-435-3
    10 Digit ISBN: 1-4165-3377-X; 13 Digit ISBN: 978-1-4165-3377-1
        1. Teenagers—Religious life. 2. Psychology, Religious. I. Ladd, Grace. II. Ladd, Joy.
    III. Title

    BV4447.L32 2005
    248.8'3—dc22

                                                                        2004060949

13 12 11 10 9 8 7 6 5 4

HOWARD colophon is a registered trademark of Simon & Schuster, Inc.

Manufactured in the United States of America

For information regarding special discounts for bulk purchases, please contact: Simon & Schuster Special Sales at 1-800-456-6798 or business@simonandschuster.com.

Edited by Michele Buckingham
Interior design by John Mark Luke Designs
Cover design by Stephanie Walker

Some of the names used in illustrations in this book are not actual names; identifying details have been changed to protect anonymity. Any resemblance is purely coincidental.

Contents

Contents

Power Principle #4: The Power of Relationship

Power Principle #5: The Power of Attitude

Power Principle #6: The Power of Faith

Power Principle #7: The Power of Courage

Acknowledgments

We would like to thank the many friends that gave us input for the content of this book. A special thanks to Kristen Fletcher, Sara Bailey, and Lane Dobrey for your wonderful ideas and creative thoughts. We enjoyed the process of working together. Thank you to Billy Steadman and Jennifer Harmon for the stories you wrote and shared for our readers.

Expect great things from God. Attempt great things for God.

—William Carey

Introduction

The Power to Make a Difference
How God Can Use You to Make a Positive Impact

*Follow anything that makes you want to do right. Pursue faith
and love and peace, and enjoy the companionship of those
who call on the Lord with pure hearts.*

—2 Timothy 2:22

Write a book with our mom? That's not how we envisioned spending the summer of 2003. We must admit, we didn't have picture-perfect, positive attitudes when we started; but then again, how many teens do? With all the pressures of school, friends, and family, a positive attitude isn't easy to come by—especially when you're between the ages of twelve and twenty. However, as we wrote this book, we began to see that it is possible to be a positive teen, even in the midst of life's struggles. Things around you don't have to be 100 percent perfect before you can have a positive attitude!

In offering this book to you, we're not pretending to have it all together. Let's face it: we're only teenagers. The main ideas in this book don't come from us; they come from the greatest source of wisdom in the world: God's Word. What we've done is searched the Scriptures for messages that apply to our lives as teens. Along with these truths, we've included stories from other teenagers and information from a variety of sources (and, of course, Mom's input) to create an all-around guide for surviving the teenage years in a positive, powerful way.

1

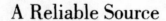

A Reliable Source

One thing we know for sure: the Bible isn't just for adults or people in the ministry. God's Word has real, everyday applications for teenagers too. Its wisdom has stood for thousands of years and is as relevant to our lives today as it was to those who lived long ago. In fact, we believe that in today's fast-paced world of "take-your-pick" philosophies and "if-it-feels-good-do-it" morals, God's Word is the only firm foundation on which to build our lives.

You will find seven biblical principles highlighted in the pages of this book—confidence, responsibility, integrity, relationship, attitude, faith, and courage—all factors that play a big role in our lives as teenagers. In each of these areas, we have the choice of responding positively or negatively. And that's what being a positive teen comes down to: making positive, godly choices in the way we react to the important issues of life.

Maybe you're wondering, *Is it really possible for me to be a positive teen? Can even a negative teenager become positive?* The answer is yes! The choice is yours. You can choose to see God's hope in the challenging situations of your life, or you can choose to grumble and complain. You can choose to allow God to work mightily in your life, or you can choose to ignore him. You can choose to build relationships, or you can choose to destroy them by your actions and words.

Every day we are faced with these kinds of choices. We've discovered that when it comes to making *positive* choices, the Bible is our best resource. Second Timothy 3:16–17 says, "All Scripture is inspired by God and is useful to teach us what is true and to make us realize what is wrong in our lives. It straightens us out and teaches us to do what is right. It is God's way of preparing us in every way, fully equipped for every good thing God wants us to do."

Every oak tree started out as a couple of nuts who stood their ground. —Author unknown

In other words, through the power of God's Word (and the work of his Holy Spirit), we can become positive teenagers who make a powerful impact in our world. After all, Jesus took a simple lunch from a young boy and fed five thousand hungry mouths. Just think what he can do with the simple gifts, talents, and abilities we have to offer! If we have positive, willing hearts that are open to the God-possibilities, there's no limit to what God can do in us and through us. We need to expect God to move!

POWER BOOST

It's our hope that the principles in these pages will be an encouragement to you and give you a powerful boost in a positive direction. You can read this book on your own or with a group of friends. At the end of each chapter, we've included a Power Point section that gives you additional scriptures to read and discuss, a prayer to pray, a verse to remember, and an activity to do by yourself or with your friends.

We pray that this book will be the beginning of a whole new perspective on life for you. Writing this book has made a positive impact on our lives; we hope reading it will make a positive impact on yours.

Through God's power and strength, you, too, can choose to be a positive teen!

THe image oF A Positive TeeN

The life each of us lives is the life within the limits of our own thinking.
To have life more abundant, we must think in limitless terms of abundance.

—Thomas Dreier

The quality of our expectations determines the quality of our action.

—André Godin

Being Positively Who You Are
But What If I Don't Feel So Positive?

Be glad for all God is planning for you.
Be patient in trouble and always be prayerful.

—Romans 12:12

How positive do you feel? Let's take a little quiz and see where you stand. Give yourself one point if the comment below makes you think, *That's definitely me.* Give yourself two points if you think, *That's sometimes me*, and three points if the comment makes you think, *That's definitely not me.* Write your points in the margin. Here we go:

- When my parents ask me to take out the trash, I think they're being annoying and roll my eyes.
- I don't always try to (cheerfully) look for the good in every situation.
- I don't jump out of bed in the morning, excited about another day of school.
- I argue with my brother, sister, and/or parents.
- There are times when I feel self-conscious and discouraged about myself.
- I let my moods affect my attitude.
- I'm not cheery, happy, and joyful 24/7.

Ready to tally your score? Just add up the numbers you wrote in the margin. How did you do? Did you get a low score? Congratulations, you're normal! We didn't do so well either. The fact is, as teenagers, we're human, and we respond to situations and circumstances in our lives in, let's just say, less-than-perfect ways. So is there hope for us? Is it possible that any of us can become positive teens, even if we don't feel like it? Even if our world is falling apart around us?

The answer is yes. Each of us has the opportunity to allow the power of God to work in our lives. All of God's attributes are positive, and he positively wants to make a difference in our lives. He loves us, and he desires to have a relationship with us. On our own, we may not be so positive; but we can find great joy in walking hand in hand with him. Consider King David in the Old Testament. Now, David was no picture-perfect, positive person. His life wasn't easy, and he made quite a few mistakes through the years. But he had a heart for God. As a result, God took a simple shepherd boy and did positive, powerful things through him. Read what David had to say about God's blessings in his life:

> I said to the LORD, "You are my Master!
>> All the good things I have are from you. . . ."
>
> LORD, you alone are my inheritance, my cup of blessing.
>> You guard all that is mine.
>
> The land you have given me is a pleasant land.
>> What a wonderful inheritance!
>
> I will bless the LORD who guides me;
>> even at night my heart instructs me.
>
> I know the LORD is always with me.
>> I will not be shaken, for he is right beside me.
>
> No wonder my heart is filled with joy,
>> and my mouth shouts his praises! (Psalm 16:2, 5–9)

Together, David and God were a positive team. And their teamwork started when David was young, long before he became a big deal

To thine own self be true, And it must follow, as the night the day, Thou canst not then be false to any man. —William Shakespeare, Hamlet

in Israel. God wants to team up to do positive things in your life too. Right now. While you're young. Does that surprise you? Often we picture God up there in the heavens, shaking his head as he looks down at us, thinking, *There they go again, messing up everything*—when, in fact, God is lovingly supporting us, redeeming us, forgiving us, and guiding us. Despite our negative tendencies, we have a positive God who is at work in our lives. He wants to fill us with joy and do amazing things in us and through us. He wants to help us become positive teens.

The Mirror

So what does a positive teen look like? Take a moment and write down some of the descriptive words that come to mind when you hear the phrase *positive teen*. Go ahead; you can write in the book. We'll leave a little space for you.

_____

_____

_____

_____

Maybe you think being positive means being perky all the time, or kind of ditzy-happy. Or maybe you think some people are just born with a positive attitude, and others simply aren't. Maybe you think the only way you could possibly become a more positive person is by faking it. None of these things are true. Being positive doesn't mean being silly or ignoring reality. It doesn't mean keeping a smile on your face through thick and thin. It means living from day to day with a contented and joyful spirit. It's a lifestyle choice each of us can make.

The question is, how are we going to allow the events of our lives to affect us, to affect our mind-set? Being a positive teen means choosing to have an optimistic outlook, because we know, as David did, that

God is right beside us. It means reflecting through our words and actions the hope and joy that we receive from God. It means seeking and running to God.

We have to admit, we forget about that hope sometimes. It's easy to fall into the rut of responding negatively to everything. What we've discovered is that we have to rely on God to fill us with his love and joy. Then we have to rely on him to help us live in a way that allows those qualities to genuinely shine through, so we don't respond to situations with a fake smile or pretend laugh.

We think that, bottom line, a positive teen can ultimately be identified by three traits:

1. A positive teen recognizes his or her need for God.
2. A positive teen makes wise choices based on what's right, not feelings.
3. A positive teen doesn't blame people or circumstances.

Let's take a closer look at each of these characteristics.

Recognizing Our Need for God

A positive teen realizes it's impossible to be positive on his or her own. Being positive is a God-thing, not an us-thing. We don't have all it takes to walk moment by moment with a positive outlook or to react in a positive way to every circumstance. We need God's positive presence in our lives. David knew his joy didn't come from himself but from God. That's why he said, "Restore to me again the joy of your salvation, and make me willing to obey you" (Psalm 51:12).

We are poor, but God is rich. He is rich with love, joy, peace, patience, kindness, goodness, faithfulness, gentleness, and self-control (see Galatians 5:22–23). All of these are positive qualities—the fruit of his Holy Spirit at work in our lives. Jesus said, "God blesses those who realize their need for him, for the kingdom of heaven is given to them" (Matthew 5:3). That, in a nutshell, is the key to being positive: recognizing that we are dependent on God for all of the positive qualities in our lives.

Think about the apostle Paul. His life circumstances were far from perfect. He was mocked, beaten, stoned, left for dead (twice), and imprisoned. If anyone could have been negative and screamed, "Life's not fair!" he could have. Yet Paul was one of the most positive people in the Bible. In fact, many of his most encouraging letters were written while he was in prison! In those letters he encouraged the early Christians to "always be joyful" and "always be thankful" (1 Thessalonians 5:16, 18).

The difficulties Paul encountered weren't the result of something he did wrong. Quite the contrary, his challenges came as a result of doing what was right: telling people about Jesus. Typically, don't we tend to think that if we're obeying God and doing what is right, nothing bad will happen to us? Wrong! Bad things happened to many of the "biggies" in the Bible (Adam, Noah, Moses, Joseph, Job, Jonah, David, Daniel—you get the idea).

Just because our life circumstances are difficult doesn't mean that God has left us. Actually, these are the times we can stand back and see the hand of God at work all the more, helping us to make it through. God doesn't promise that our lives will go smoothly; he promises that he will be with us in the midst of our struggles. He will never leave us. Listen to the promise God gave to his precious people back in the time of Isaiah the prophet:

> But now, O Israel, the LORD who created you says: "Do not be afraid, for I have ransomed you. I have called you by name; you are mine. When you go through deep waters and great trouble, I will be with you. When you go through rivers of difficulty, you will not drown! When you walk through the fire of oppression you will not be burned up; the flames will not consume you. For I am the

LORD, your God, the Holy One of Israel, your Savior. . . . You are precious to me. You are honored, and I love you.

"Do not be afraid, for I am with you." (Isaiah 43:1–5)

We can walk in confidence that God is with us and make the best of our circumstances, even when they're difficult. In Paul's case, his prison cell became his writing room and ministry headquarters. What about your life? Have you ever felt defeated and discouraged, like you were in a prison cell? Have you ever felt like giving up because all the doors seemed to be shut or because you thought you'd made too many mistakes? Well, there's hope! God is with you, just as he was with Paul and David. And he can take the broken pieces of your life, along with your gifts and abilities, mix them together, and use them all in a wonderful and positive way. As Romans 8:28 tells us, "we can know that God causes everything to work together for the good of those who love God and are called according to his purpose for them."

The Power to Choose

"But I don't feel like it!" How many times have you said those words? Thankfully, when it comes to being a positive teen, we don't have to *feel* positive in order to *be* positive.

Maybe you're thinking, *But aren't we being fake if we act positive when we don't feel that way?* Stop and think about that question for a moment. If we always waited until we felt like doing something before we did it, we'd never get much done! Do we live by our feelings, or do we do what is right? (The feelings usually follow.) Should our feelings really determine how we act or think?

What if your dad said, "I don't feel like going to work anymore, so I won't"? Your family's lifestyle would change dramatically—and you probably wouldn't like the new picture. What if your mom said, "I don't feel like doing the laundry this year, so I won't"? You'd either have to learn how to use the Tide yourself, or you'd have to wear smelly clothes for the next twelve months. What if the lifeguard at the pool looked down at a struggling swimmer and said, "I don't feel like jumping in and getting wet right now"? In that case, feelings could mean the difference between life and death!

Life demands that we not determine our actions by our feelings. So when we want to say, "But I just don't feel like being positive!" what we really need to ask ourselves is, "How can I choose to be positive in this situation, whether I feel like it or not?" Personally, we're always amazed at how positive we feel once we make a decision to act or say something positive.

Take smiling, for instance. Smiles are something we often associate with naturally cheerful and positive people. But we can *choose* to smile. We're not suggesting that we should smile all the time; there are definitely times when we need to grieve and cry. But there are also many times when we miss the opportunity to put on a smile—not a fake smile, but a real one offered as a gift to the people around us. A smile is a present that we give to people, knowing that it lifts their day. Smiles are based on what we choose to do for someone else, not on "me, me, me" and how *we* feel right now.

A smile is the universal language that speaks a thousand words. It says, "I'm glad to see you," "You're important," "I'm thankful," "It's going to be all right." One man put it this way, "A smile will go a long way, but you will have to start it on its journey."[1]

Choosing to smile is one positive decision that's relatively easy to make. But moment by moment, day by day, we face many choices that basically come down to this: will we choose to do what is right, or will we follow our feelings? Will we choose to:

- encourage others rather than tear them down?
- pray more and worry less?
- courageously stand up for what is right instead of cowering in fear?

Be honest in your estimate of yourselves, measuring your value by how much faith God has given you. —Romans 12:3

- live a life of integrity instead of dishonesty?
- love all people with God's love rather than hate the people we don't like?
- fill our hearts and minds with contentment instead of bitterness and anger?

We're not saying we should ignore our feelings. But we *are* saying that feelings shouldn't dominate our behavior. *We* are in control of what we say, do, and think—not our feelings. Thankfully we are blessed with the power to choose how we will respond to whatever life brings. Our response is our responsibility.

The Blame Game

We often want to blame other people for our negative responses. It's easy to throw blame at someone else and deflect the responsibility for our choices off our own backs. But the truth is, blaming others is the exact opposite of being positive. It only leads to bitterness and anger.

Right now, stop and think: what is your most common reason—or excuse—for being negative?

- "My family doesn't have enough money."
- "That teacher doesn't like me."
- "My parents grounded me."
- "The new girl in class annoys me."
- "I'm not as good-looking as the other girls (or guys)."
- "Coach didn't pick me for the basketball team."
- "No one understands me."
- "_____." (You fill in the blank.)

Excuses are a dime a dozen. Unfortunately, excuses only cripple us and stifle us from becoming the positive teens God wants us to be. Blaming freezes our potential and zaps our energy.

One teenager, Robin (not her real name), is a good example of this. She is a grumbling and negative person; and if you ask her, she'll tell you exactly why. Her dad died of a heart attack when she was in high school, her mother was never there for her, and her brother spent the next several years on drugs. She's mad at the world, and it shows. She refuses to crack a smile and complains about everything she can. And she certainly doesn't bless other people with her actions or attitude! Instead, Robin stays busy nursing all her hurts and blaming everyone else for the way she lives. Instead of forgiving the people who hurt her when she was younger, she uses them as an excuse for not living for Christ and making positive choices today.

Are there people you need to forgive? All of us must ask ourselves that question. Instead of blaming others for our negative attitudes, we need to make the positive decision to forgive those people who've hurt us. As Christians, it's our responsibility to forgive, since we have been freely forgiven by God. Ultimately, forgiving others is one of the most positive things we can do—for them and for us.

Sometimes we don't blame people; we blame circumstances. But that's a dead end too. The excuses, "I can't because . . . ," "It's not my fault," or "If only . . ." won't get us too far down the road toward living positive lives. We need to remember: no matter what we're facing, God is with us. That means there is always a glimmer of hope in every circumstance. We just have to find it! Instead of blaming our circumstances and wallowing in discouragement and defeat, we need to search for the positive possibilities in the midst of our circumstances, move forward in hope, and keep our eyes open for what God can teach us through the situation.

That's what sixteen-year-old Carla did. Her dad didn't make as much money as some of her friends' dads, and that made her feel angry. But instead of staying mad or stewing about the situation with a sorry attitude, she did something positive. She found a job, knowing that she could help her family and that God could teach her many things through her work. Now Carla is learning the value of a solid work ethic, developing a sense of responsibility, and getting many opportunities to shine for Christ—all as a result of having to get a job.

Track-and-field legend Wilma Rudolph is another positive person who refused to get caught up in the blame game. Growing up, she faced many difficult circumstances; but she moved beyond blame to live a life of joy, discipline, accomplishment, and Olympic victory.

In 1940 Wilma was born prematurely; and as if that didn't cause enough struggle, she contracted double pneumonia and scarlet fever. Later a bout with polio left her with a crooked leg and a foot that was twisted inward. As a result, Wilma spent most of her childhood in braces.

Wilma's adversity generated a determined spirit within her. By the age of eleven, she was sneaking around without the braces. When she told her doctor what she had been doing, the doctor acquiesced and said it was OK for her to not wear the braces "sometimes." In Wilma's mind, "sometimes" meant "never again." By thirteen, Wilma was on her school basketball and track teams. Two years later she was chosen to participate in a summer sports camp with the Tennessee State University Tigerbelles. There, a teammate got her interested in running for the U.S. Olympic team.

During the 1956 Olympics, at the age of sixteen, Wilma reached the semifinals in the 200-meter dash and won a bronze medal as a member of the women's 400-meter relay team. Her heart was set on winning a gold medal, though, so she determined to run again in the 1960 Olympics. For the next four years Wilma underwent a rigorous training program, even as she paid her own way through Tennessee State University and maintained a B average in her studies.

When the 1960 Olympics started, Wilma was ready. She won the hearts of eighty thousand fans as she ran her way to three gold medals—the first American woman to win three gold medals in Olympic track-and-field history.[2] Few Olympians have matched Wilma's determination and perseverance against such odds. Because she made the positive choice to look beyond her circumstances and see the possibilities, she became an inspiration to us all.

Do you want to become a positive teen? Then start today by recognizing your need for God. You can't be positive without him; it's not in you. It's not in any of us! Then begin to make wise choices based on what's right, not on how you feel at any particular moment. Finally, stop blaming other people or your circumstances for the way you respond to life. Choose to forgive. Choose to see God's hand at work. Choose to be a positive teen!

POWER POINT

⬡ **Read:** Genesis 37:1–4, 18–28, and 50:14–21. What opportunities did Joseph have to blame others? (You can skim Genesis 39 and 40 for more about Joseph's life.) How does Joseph's response demonstrate someone with positive qualities?

⬤ **Pray:** Perfect heavenly Father, I praise you for your greatness and power. I praise you for your loving-kindness and mercy toward me. Thank you for working in my life in a powerful way. Thank you for being with me in the good times and the rough ones. It is wonderful to know that you will never leave me. Help me to rise above excuses and blaming. Give me the ability and discernment to make positive choices throughout my life in all of my words, actions, and attitudes. Most importantly, allow me to glorify you through the choices that I make. In Jesus's name, amen.

♀ **Remember:** Romans 12:12: "Be glad for all God is planning for you. Be patient in trouble, and always be prayerful."

☺ **Do:** Take some time to think about the people and things you tend to blame in your life. Prayerfully forgive each person against whom you are holding a grudge. Recognize that you must move on, no longer allowing that person or what they did to hold you in bondage. If you are in a difficult circumstance, don't allow it to be an excuse in your life. Look beyond your circumstances, asking God to show you the hope through the difficulties.

Finally, recognize that being a positive teen takes the combination of one perfect God and one not-so-perfect teenager who recognizes his or her need for God. Decide today to make positive choices that will allow God to do powerful things in you and through you.

Is It Totally Up to Me?
God's Power at Work in You

I have often wished that I were a more devout man than I am. Nevertheless, amid the greatest difficulties of my administration, when I could not see any other resort, I would place my whole reliance on God, knowing that all would go well, and that He would decide for the right.

—Abraham Lincoln

Don't you just hate it when the battery runs out? Whether it's the TV remote, a cell phone, or a portable CD player, it's always frustrating to press the power button and get nothing!

Sometimes we feel that way ourselves—no power to perform, no pizzazz to keep going, no perk for enjoying life. We're not talking about being physically worn out, although that can play a part in our motivation to get moving. We're talking about lacking the *internal* power to live life abundantly and to its fullest potential.

The bad news is that all of us feel burned-out sometimes. The good news is that we have a spiritual power source that is always available to us. In fact, the same power-filled God who created the universe wants to work in our lives in a power-filled way. He loves us and doesn't just leave us here on earth to try to live in our own strength.

Take a look at what Peter had to say when he wrote to the early Christians about God's power. Remember, Peter was a big, burly fisherman who had physical strength and stamina. But he also recognized that he needed God's power at work in his life:

As we know Jesus better, his divine power gives us everything we need for living a godly life. He has called us to receive his own glory and goodness! And by that same mighty power, he has given us all of his rich and wonderful promises. He has promised that you will escape the decadence all around you caused by evil desires and that you will share in his divine nature. (2 Peter 1:3–4)

Did you read that? *Really* read it? Think about it: as we get to know Jesus better, his divine power gives us *everything* we need for living a godly life—not just part of what we need, but the total package. And think about this: it's God's amazing, overwhelming, exceedingly wonderful *divine power*, not flimsy people power, that gives us these things. By his power, God also gives us all of his rich promises, including the promise that we—mere teenagers—can actually share in his divine nature! So whether we are at school or the mall, or with friends, we really can live for God. We have no excuse not to.

What's Our Part?

Peter didn't stop at verse 4, however. He realized that we must do *our* part by making an effort to appropriate God's power. We can't just sit around like couch potatoes, waiting for God's divine power to pour through us. We have to get up and *do* something. Here's what Peter said in verses 5–8:

So make every effort to apply the benefits of these promises to your life. Then your faith will produce a life of moral excellence. A life of moral excellence leads to knowing God better. Knowing God leads to self-control. Self-control leads to patient endurance, and patient endurance leads to godliness. Godliness leads to love for other Christians, and finally you will grow to have genuine love for everyone. The more you grow like this, the more you will become productive and useful in your knowledge of our Lord Jesus Christ.

Now that's a wonderful description of a positive teen, isn't it? But notice, Peter didn't say God's intent is to zap us with his power and make us instantly perfect. In fact, Peter didn't say that we have to be perfect at all. He simply said we have to make an effort to apply God's promises to our lives. And as we do, one thing will lead to another. Moral excellence will lead to a better understanding of God, which will lead to self-control, which will lead to patience. The next step in the progression is godliness, which will lead to love for our Christian brothers and sisters and eventually for everyone. It's a process of growth. According to Peter, if we grow this way we will become "productive and useful in the knowledge of our Lord Jesus Christ." Productive and useful teenagers! That's what *we* would love to be. How about you?

Personally, we're glad Peter began this whole power passage by reminding us that God is the one who gives us the power and ability to grow in our spiritual lives. We simply need to make every effort we can to walk down that road of growth and experience. And the wonderful blessing about God's power is that it never runs out. Ephesians 3:20 gives us tremendous encouragement: "Now glory be to God! By his mighty power at work within us, he is able to accomplish infinitely more than we would ever dare to ask or hope."

It's truly sad when people choose false power sources instead of God's loving, everlasting power. Recently we met a young man who was struggling spiritually and searching for answers. Here's how the story unfolded: I (Grace) had just returned from a mission trip in Guatemala, and I was tired and hungry. So on the way home, after Mom and I dropped off my pictures from the trip to be developed, we stopped at a deli to have a bagel. We rarely went to this place, and we had just missed the breakfast crowd. Since we were the only ones in the section, our waiter stopped and talked with us for quite a while.

Darren (not his real name) told us that he had just gotten out of prison. His life was "all screwed up," he said. He had tried just about everything, but he still felt his life had no meaning or direction. He got his "power and energy" from his drug habit. The problem was, the drugs only provided a temporary fix. He always had to face himself again the next day.

Obviously Darren was unhappy and searching. When we told him that we found our joy, power, and strength from God, he said that he'd grown up in Russia, where people didn't talk about God much. Then he remembered: he did have one friend who'd made a decision to put his faith in God—a step that changed his friend's life for the better.

"All of my friends are messed up, except that one," he admitted.

Darren gave us lots of excuses to explain why he couldn't follow God. He said that since he couldn't see God, he had a hard time believing in him. He complained that he just couldn't understand the Bible, so we began asking him some questions and working through his excuses.

"Is your life working for you right now?" we asked. He couldn't honestly say that it was.

Darren was the picture of a young man who'd chosen to pursue a false sense of energy and strength from a false power source, and that choice was only leading him toward destruction and death. Our hearts ached for the joyful, productive, and useful life we knew he was missing.

Later, the three of us went back to visit Darren again at the deli. He remembered us and wanted to talk to us (as much as he could between waiting tables). We gave him a Bible in an easy-to-understand translation and encouraged him to read it. We don't know what will happen with Darren, but at least we know we've helped in a small way to direct him toward the One who can help him find true power and hope.

She Found It

Darren's story reminds us of another person's story. The so-called woman at the well (her story is found in John 4 in the Bible) was a woman who had tried it all. She tried to divert Jesus with excuses, just as Darren did with us. The woman came to the well to draw water intended to refresh her body; but Jesus offered her living water so her heart would thirst no more.

The Bible says that while the disciples were in town buying food, Jesus approached the well and asked the Samaritan woman to give him a drink. As you read the following passage (John 4:9–26), keep in mind that Jews despised Samaritans:

> She said to Jesus, "You are a Jew, and I am a Samaritan woman, why are you asking me for a drink?"
>
> Jesus replied, "If you only knew the gift God has for you and who I am, you would ask me and I would give you living water."
>
> "But sir, you don't have a rope or a bucket," she said, "and this is a very deep well. Where would you get this living water? And besides, are you greater than our ancestor Jacob who gave us this well? How can you offer better water than he and his sons and his cattle enjoyed?" *[Hmmm. If this woman seems a bit confused now, just wait.]*
>
> Jesus replied, "People soon become thirsty again after drinking this water. But the water I give them takes away thirst altogether. It becomes a perpetual spring within them, giving them eternal life."
>
> "Please, sir," the woman said, "give me some of that water! Then I'll never be thirsty again, and I won't have to come here to

haul water." *[Obviously, this woman and Jesus are not on the same page!]*

"Go and get your husband," Jesus told her.

"I don't have a husband," the woman replied.

Jesus said, "You're right! You don't have a husband—for you have had five husbands, and you aren't even married to the man you're living with now." *[Uh-oh. The conversation is getting downright embarrassing.]*

"Sir," the woman said, "you must be a prophet. So tell me why is it that you Jews insist that Jerusalem is the only place of worship, while we Samaritans claim it is here at Mount Gerizim, where our ancestors worshiped?" *[Good move—create a distraction.]*

Jesus replied, "Believe me, the time is coming when it will no longer matter whether you worship the Father here or in Jerusalem. You Samaritans know so little about the one you worship, while we Jews know all about him, for salvation comes through the Jews. But the time is coming and is already here when true worshipers will worship the Father in spirit and in truth. The Father is looking for anyone who will worship him that way. For God is Spirit, so those who worship him must worship in spirit and in truth." *[Jesus lovingly brings everything back to basics.]*

The woman said, "I know the Messiah will come—the one who is called Christ. When he comes, he will explain everything to us." *[OK, now she's getting it!]*

Then Jesus told her, "I am the Messiah." *[There it is—plain as day. Jesus says he is the one true Messiah!]*

Over the centuries, people have argued that Jesus was a good man, a prophet, or a great teacher. But look at Jesus's statement in John 4:26. He was either the Messiah (God's Son and mankind's Savior), or he was a baldfaced liar. Which do you choose to believe? Have you met the Messiah? Jesus came to this world to offer his life for us. God lovingly gave his only Son, Jesus, so that whoever believes in him will not perish for the wrong things he or she has done, but instead will have eternal life in heaven (see John 3:16).

As we enter into a faith relationship with Jesus, he not only offers forgiveness; he offers living water. He offers his Spirit to nourish our souls and give us strength and power to live abundant and productive lives. Some of us may choose to cover our hurts, deny our guilt, and find other ways to "feel good." But God's living water is the only true, never-ending source of refreshment that ensures that we will thirst no more. Just as the woman at the well came to Jesus with a tattered and scarred life, so Jesus meets us right where we are and offers hope. His living power at work in our lives is greater than any other resource available to us.

A New Life

The woman at the well left her encounter with Jesus with a new hope and a new life. She had met the God who loved her, and his power changed her forever. Her past sins were forgiven, and her direction was changed. She ran to tell all the people in her town about what happened to her, and many received hope from Jesus that day.

As teenagers, we often place our trust in false power sources—whether people or drugs or popularity or grades or material things. The problem is, all these resources will eventually run out. Or we'll continue to need more and more of them just to (barely) survive. False sources of strength only lead to despair. But God is a God of hope. He can take a life filled with pain and destruction and restore it with redemption and new life. He can work in a mighty way through us, despite our weaknesses and failings. The same resurrection power that

The basic difference between physical and spiritual power is that men use physical power, but spiritual power uses men. —Justin Wroe Nixon

raised Christ from the dead is available to work in *our* lives (see Romans 8:11). And the wonderful thing about God's love and power is that it comes from a well that will never run dry. We may fail a test, our money may run out, a friend may betray us; but God will not abandon us. His love and power are extended to us continually.

The early Christians knew the wonder of God's power at work in them. Before he ascended to heaven, Jesus told his followers: "When the Holy Spirit has come upon you, you will receive power and will tell people about me everywhere—in Jerusalem, throughout Judea, in Samaria, and to the ends of the earth" (Acts 1:8). And they did! Through this ragtag team of people, God spread his message of truth throughout the world. But they were not alone. Jesus gave them the greatest gift he could when he left this world: part of himself to dwell in them. Wow! We should be awed by this! The whole book of Acts is a testament to the fact that God's Holy Spirit moved powerfully through the disciples' strengths and weaknesses, successes and failures.

What can God do through us? After all, we're just teenagers. But the same power that raised Jesus from the dead is available to us today. Our age isn't the issue. The only issue is, do we believe? Are we followers of Jesus? There is hope and power through Christ. Never underestimate what God can do through a generation of positive teens who place their hope and trust in him!

POWER POINT

Read: 2 Corinthians 12:9–10. What does this passage tell us about God's power? Are our weaknesses a problem to God? Now read Romans 8:35–39. What can separate us from God's love? Where is our victory?

Pray: Wonderful, powerful heavenly Father, to think that you are the Creator of the universe, the Maker of mankind, and yet you want to work in a powerful way in my life! Thank you! Praise you! Pour your power through my life, as you work through both my strengths and my weaknesses. Energize my life with your Spirit. Help me to live a godly and productive life. Direct me down your pathways as I seek to honor you. In Jesus's name I pray, amen.

⚲ **Remember:** 2 Peter 1:3: "As we know Jesus better, his divine power gives us everything we need for living a godly life. He has called us to receive his own glory and goodness!"

☺ **Do:** Have you placed your hope and trust in Christ? John 1:12 tells us, "To all who believed him [Jesus] and accepted him, he gave the right to become children of God." When we put our faith in Jesus, we become precious children of the King, and his resurrection power is available to us. Have you ever come to that point of decision—a specific time in your life when you realized you wanted a relationship with God and the assurance that you would go to heaven when you die? Jesus came to earth to give us that assurance. He offered his life on the cross as a sacrifice for our sins, and his resurrection gives us the hope of eternal life.

All God asks of us is to believe in Christ Jesus as our Savior. Ephesians 2:8–10 says, "God saved you by his special favor when you believed. And you can't take credit for this; it is a gift from God. Salvation is not a reward for the good things we have done, so none of us can boast about it. For we are God's masterpiece. He has created us anew in Christ Jesus, so that we can do the good things he planned for us long ago."

Would you take a moment right now to consider placing your faith and trust in Christ? If you have already placed your faith in him, use this time to thank Jesus for his work in your life. Ask him to continue to work in a powerful way through you.

Power Principle #1

THe Power OF Confidence

For God has not given us a spirit of fear and timidity, but of power, love, and self-discipline.

—2 Timothy 1:7

Never bend your head. Hold it high. Look the world straight in the eye.

—Helen Keller

Perfect Creation
God Doesn't Make Mistakes

You made all the delicate, inner parts of my body and knit me together in my mother's womb. Thank you for making me so wonderfully complex! Your workmanship is marvelous—and how well I know it.

—Psalm 139:13–14

Perfect creation? We know what you're thinking: *You've got to be kidding! Doesn't everyone have flaws? Don't we all have things we wish we could change about ourselves?* Let's go ahead and admit it: most teenagers—no, most people—struggle with accepting certain things about themselves. Whether physically, mentally, or personality-wise, we all have a few things we would love to tweak, redo, or change. The question is, do these flaws represent glitches in the creation process, or did God give us these traits by design? Did God truly intend for each of us to come out the way we are?

Several years ago Mom bought a small, silver purse decorated with imbedded gemstones. It was truly unique and beautiful, but it came with a note that read something like this: "This product is a designer original. Each purse is handmade and may contain slight imperfections, which only serve to add to its beauty and originality." Perhaps we all need to view ourselves with that label! We are designer originals, created by the all-wise and loving God of the universe. Even our little imperfections serve to add to our unique beauty.

That's not just what we think—that's what God's Word says. David wrote in Psalm 139:13–17:

You made all the delicate inner parts of my body

and knit me together in my mother's womb.

Thank you for making me so wonderfully complex!

Your workmanship is marvelous—and how well I know it.

You watched me as I was being formed in utter seclusion,

as I was woven together in the dark of the womb.

You saw me before I was born.

Every day of my life was recorded in your book.

Every moment was laid out

before a single day had passed.

How precious are your thoughts about me, O God!

They are innumerable!

Original Design versus Free Will

God made us exactly the way he wanted to make us. But he also created us with a free will. As teenagers we make certain choices that affect our inward and outward appearance—and we're not talking about deciding whether or not to get a nose job. We're talking about how we act and respond. Take our personalities, for instance. Yes, God made us with certain tendencies (like being quiet and passive or outgoing and active), but we make the choice to have a negative and self-centered attitude or a positive and selfless one. And that choice affects how other people see us—and how we see ourselves. We can't have an obnoxious, annoyingly selfish attitude and then make the excuse, "Well, that's just the way God made me!" We have choices. We need to accept and be happy with who we are, without recklessly abandoning the responsibility to be the best we can be.

It's an easy temptation to live at the level of our lowest self (also known as our sinful nature), sit back and make no effort to be our best, and then blame who we are on God. "That's just the way God made me" is a lame excuse for selfishness, anger, laziness, and a host of other "flaws." Ephesians 2:10 tells us we are God's workmanship, but it doesn't stop there. It also reminds us that we're created in Christ to do positive things: "For we are God's masterpiece. He has created us anew in Christ Jesus, so that we can do *the good things* he planned for us long ago" (emphasis added).

Yes, God created us just the way he intended for us to be. We are his masterpieces, and even our imperfections serve a far greater, eternal purpose than we know. But we still have to choose to do "the good things" he has planned for our lives. With thankfulness, we have to acknowledge that God has a plan for us and that he can work through both our strengths and our weaknesses.

Content with Our Weaknesses?

Perhaps you're thinking, *Yeah, right. You don't know my weaknesses. How can I be thankful and happy about them? And how can God possibly work through me as long as I'm this way?*

Maybe you were born with a physical handicap or disability. To a certain extent, we all have handicaps. We all have weak spots. We can't do everything well. (OK, OK, we know—there are always a couple of people at school who seem to succeed in everything. But even *they* have something they can't do; it's just harder to identify what it is.) Whether great or small, our weaknesses and handicaps can tend to get us down if we let them. And when our eyes are focused on our weaknesses, it's impossible to be positive teens.

When we're hung up on our handicaps, here are three things we can do:

1. Focus on our strengths. By focusing on our strengths, we minimize our weaknesses. We need to concentrate on what we *can* do and do it to the best of our ability.

If God had wanted me otherwise, He would have created me otherwise. —Johann von Goethe

2. Don't compare ourselves with others. God has a different plan and path for every person. We need to keep our eyes on the track God has chosen for us and not worry about what someone else is doing. As our mother, a former track coach, used to tell her runners, "Keep your eyes on the finish line. If you focus on the other runners, it will only slow you down."

3. Ask God to work through our weaknesses. He may not take away our disability or challenge, but he can give us strength in spite of it. In fact, he can do mighty things *through* it.

How can we say that God will work through our weaknesses? Remember, the apostle Paul talked about having a "thorn in the flesh" in 2 Corinthians 12:7–10. We don't know exactly what that "thorn" was, because Paul chose not to identify it. Some theologians speculate that it was perhaps malaria, epilepsy, or a disease of the eyes. Whatever it was, it was a chronic, debilitating condition that sometimes hindered Paul's work. He prayed for its removal, but God didn't take it away. Why not? Paul's "thorn" had a great purpose in his life. Since Paul was a strong, self-sufficient man in many ways, this thorn in his flesh kept him humble and dependent on God.

"Three different times I begged the Lord to take it away," he wrote. "Each time he said, 'My gracious favor is all you need. My power works best in your weakness.' So now I am glad to boast about my weaknesses, so that the power of Christ may work through me" (2 Corinthians 12:8–9).

Be *glad* about weaknesses? That doesn't seem logical. But then, our loving heavenly Father doesn't work according to man's logic. We think God should operate through our strengths, but he wants to work even through our weaknesses and disabilities! That's why someone like Helen Keller (who was blind and deaf from an early age), could say, "I thank God for my handicaps, for through them, I have found myself, my work, and my God." [1]

Why We Don't Like Ourselves

Let's be honest. Sometimes we feel bad about ourselves because of our weaknesses. But more often than not, we're not down because of the way God created us; we're down because of our own choices. When we choose to stay angry with our parents, backstab a friend, or cheat on a test, for example, we don't like ourselves.

Don't think you're alone if you have this kind of low self-esteem. We all struggle with it from time to time. Why? Because we're all sinful people. We all make mistakes. We all make negative choices that cause us to frown when we look at our own faces in the mirror.

The good news is, we can replace our low self-esteem with Christ-esteem. You see, despite all our weaknesses and sin, God chooses to love us. He loves us so much that he sent his Son to die for us. Because of what Jesus did on the cross, we can have a relationship with our wonderful, redeeming heavenly Father, who forgives our sins and pulls us out of the pit (Psalm 103:4 NIV). And we can take comfort in the words Paul wrote in Romans 5:3–11:

> We can rejoice, too, when we run into problems and trials, for we know that they are good for us—they help us learn to endure. And endurance develops strength of character in us, and character strengthens our confident expectation of salvation. And this expectation will not disappoint us. For we know how dearly God loves us, because he has given us the Holy Spirit to fill our hearts with his love.
>
> When we were utterly helpless, Christ came at just the right time and died for us sinners. Now, no one is likely to die for a good

person, though someone might be willing to die for a person who is especially good. But God showed his great love for us by sending Christ to die for us while we were still sinners.

And since we have been made right in God's sight by the blood of Christ, he will certainly save us from God's judgment. For since we were restored to friendship with God by the death of his Son while we were still his enemies, we will certainly be delivered from eternal punishment by his life. So now we can rejoice in our wonderful new relationship with God—all because of what our Lord Jesus Christ has done for us in making us friends of God.

Yes, we can rejoice—not because we're perfect and always make positive choices, but because God loves us and redeems us, despite our imperfection. In his eyes, we have great value and worth. How can we be down on what God has redeemed at such a huge price?

Learning to Love Ourselves

Frankly, many of us need to learn to love ourselves. Easier said than done, right? But really, it's not so much about loving ourselves as it is about loving *Christ* in ourselves. Here are four steps that can help:

1. Stop focusing on ourselves. Whenever we dwell on "me, myself, and I," it's easy to get discouraged. We may think we hate ourselves; but the truth is, we're really just overly focused on *us*. We need to turn our focus in a new direction: toward God and others.

2. Serve other people. One of the best medicines for curing the I-don't-like-myself disease is showing love and kindness toward others, especially those in need. Jesus told us our two top priorities in life are to love God and then love other people (Matthew 22:37–39). As we focus on loving God and helping others, we have little time to mope about ourselves.

What can we do? Serving can involve something as simple as mak-

Do not wish to be anything but what you are. —Saint Francis de Sales

ing a phone call, sending a note, helping with a project, lending a listening ear, or offering a kind smile. Personally, we've discovered that a tremendous, joyful feeling rises up inside us whenever we reach out to help and encourage another person. For example, on a recent missions trip, I (Grace) had the opportunity to visit with homeless people in New Orleans. I talked with them and encouraged them. Most of them just wanted a friend, and I was able to be that for them. And in the process of bringing them Christ's love, I felt incredible joy. What a blessing!

3. Change bad habits or unproductive lifestyles. As we've said, we often don't like ourselves because of our own choices. Whether it's overeating, being lazy, or disobeying the law, doing something we know we shouldn't do makes it hard for us to feel good about ourselves. Sometimes we just need to regroup, identify the bad habits or lifestyles that are causing us trouble, and make the necessary changes to our lives. We can't change in our own strength, however. We need to ask God for his power and strength to be wise and self-controlled (really, *God*-controlled). We also need to ask someone we trust and respect to help us and hold us accountable.

4. Turn our focus heavenward. Just after the Last Supper, Jesus said some important words that he wanted his disciples to grasp before he left his ministry on earth: "I have loved you even as the Father has loved me. Remain in my love. When you obey me, you remain in my love, just as I obey my Father and remain in his love. I have told you this so that you will be filled with my joy. Yes, your joy will overflow!" (John 15:9–11).

We can have overflowing joy! All we have to do is put our faith in the God who loves us and created us for a purpose, and walk with him in obedience. It's a matter of focus. Will we choose to focus on ourselves and our own plans for our lives, or will we choose to focus on God and his plans for our lives? Will we choose to focus on what we want and what we need, or will we choose to focus on the needs of others, pouring out God's love to them? Will we choose to shine the light of Christ into a dark world, or will we choose to be overly consumed with ourselves?

The choice is ours every day—and it determines whether or not we're going to be positive teens. May we choose wisely!

POWER POINT

Read: Psalm 103. How does God view you? Underline the verses that specifically speak to you about the way God sees you.

Pray: Wonderful, loving Creator, I praise you for your wisdom and power evidenced in creation. Your work is marvelous! I'm grateful that the powerful God who created the vast universe down to the smallest atomic detail also carefully designed me. Thank you for the way you have made me. Thank you for the good parts of me, and thank you for the parts that I don't like so much. Help me not to get down on myself but to remember that I am a designer original, created to do good things with my life. In Jesus's name I pray, amen.

Remember: Psalm 139:14: "Thank you for making me so wonderfully complex! Your workmanship is marvelous—and how well I know it."

Do: Don't just sit there; *do* something—for someone else. Think of something you can do right now that would help another person or brighten someone's day. Maybe it's a phone call, a note, or a small act of kindness or service. Go do it! You will be amazed at how good you feel about yourself when you focus your attention on helping others.

Profound Purpose
What Can You Become?

We are God's masterpiece. He has created us anew in Christ Jesus, so
that we can do the good things he planned for us long ago.

—Ephesians 2:10

Corrie ten Boom, concentration camp survivor and author of *The*
Hiding Place, stood before an audience to share how God worked
powerfully in her life. She held up a ladies' white evening glove and
asked the audience, "What can a glove do?" As the crowd sat in silence,
she continued:

> The glove can do nothing. Oh, but if my hand is in the glove,
> it can do many things . . . cook, play the piano, write. Well, you say
> that is not the glove; that it is the hand in the glove that does it. Yes,
> that is so. I tell you that we are nothing but gloves. The hand in the
> glove is the Holy Spirit of God. Can the glove do something if it is
> very near the hand? No! The glove must be filled with the hand to
> do the work. That is exactly the same for us: We must be filled with
> the Holy Spirit to do the work God has for us to do.[1]

How many times have you asked yourself, "What can I do?" Most
of us experience some time in our lives when we feel we just can't do
anything right. Corrie's illustration relates to every Christian's life, but
especially to teens. The glove has a certain purpose, and the hand

empowers it to carry out its purpose. God has created each of us with certain gifts, talents, and abilities, and he empowers us to carry out the plans he has for us. There is a purpose to our existence. God's power through us allows us to do great work for his kingdom.

In his *New York Times* bestseller, *The Purpose-Driven Life*, Rick Warren shares that we were created for a purpose. "The purpose of your life is far greater than your own personal fulfillment, your peace of mind, or even your happiness," he writes. "It's far greater than your family, your career, or even your wildest dreams and ambitions. If you want to know why you were placed on this planet, you must begin with God. You were born by his purpose and for his purpose."[2] As teenagers, our purpose in life goes far beyond ourselves. God has a bigger plan— a plan that includes eternity.

God's Plan and Our Potential

How do we know what direction to go in life? That's a valid question for any teen, since so much of life is ahead of us. Personally, we find great comfort in knowing that God has a plan and a direction prepared for us. Jeremiah 29:11–14 offers a wonderful assurance: "'I know the plans I have for you,' says the LORD. 'They are plans for good and not for disaster, to give you a future and a hope. In those days when you pray, I will listen. If you look for me in earnest, you will find me when you seek me. I will be found by you,' says the LORD."

Isn't it amazing to think that the Creator of the universe wants us to seek him? Jesus affirmed this in the New Testament when he told his followers, "Ask and it will be given to you; seek and you will find; knock and the door will be opened to you. For everyone who asks receives; he who seeks finds; and to him who knocks, the door will be opened" (Matthew 7:7–8 NIV).

How could we ignore such a divine invitation? But the truth is, we

More men fail through lack of purpose than through lack of talent. —Billy Sunday

do! Thinking we know what's best for our own lives, we forge ahead on our own path, trusting in ourselves. We focus on the first part of Jeremiah 29 about God's plan for our lives; but rarely do we read further, to the part that tells us that when we pray, God will listen; and if we seek him earnestly, we will find him. God *wants* to lead and direct us. The question is, are we looking to him for that guidance, or are we aimlessly wandering, hoping to figure life out on our own? Maybe we're waiting for God to flash all the answers right in front of us!

Thankfully, God doesn't give us the whole plan of our lives all at once. Can you imagine if Moses or Joseph or Paul or Corrie ten Boom had known the exact plan for their lives at an early age? They probably would have given up out of pure fear! But God graciously and lovingly leads us along, one step at a time. God knows both our plan and our potential. We can't even begin to know and understand all that God can and will do through us, and that's OK it's not our job to know the future; it's our job to faithfully follow God, and he will direct our steps.

The book of Proverbs is full of reminders that God has a bigger plan than what we can see from our own little earthbound perspective. Take a look at the following verses:

- Proverbs 3:5–6: "Trust in the LORD with all your heart; do not depend on your own understanding. Seek his will in all you do, and he will direct your paths."
- Proverbs 16:3–4: "Commit your work to the LORD, and then your plans will succeed. The LORD has made everything for his own purposes."
- Proverbs 16:9: "We can make our plans, but the LORD determines our steps."
- Proverbs 19:21: "You can make many plans, but the LORD's purpose will prevail."

- Proverbs 20:24: "How can we understand the road we travel? It is the LORD who directs our steps."

How does God's direction work? Well, take our mom's career path, for example. Mom set out to be a school teacher. She was particularly talented in math, so she became a middle-school math teacher. After teaching math for several years, however, she stopped teaching to stay at home with her kids (us!). She began using her creative teacher gift in a unique way: she planned fun, creative birthday parties for us as we grew up. Without fail, at every party someone would comment to her, "You really should write a book."

Eventually, Mom did write a book about creative party planning. Later the doors opened for her to write another book, and then another, and then another. Before long, Mom the math teacher became Mom the writer. God had a different plan, a much bigger plan than she had ever imagined. Her job wasn't to know the whole plan and set her own course to it. Her job was to walk faithfully with God, seeking him and his plan.

In a prayer of brokenness the prophet Jeremiah uttered these words, "I know, LORD, that a person's life is not his own. No one is able to plan his own course" (Jeremiah 10:23). Solomon put it this way: "We may throw the dice, but the LORD determines how they fall" (Proverbs 16:33).

Concerned about the direction of your life? Join the club! The good news is, we don't have to figure it all out. All we have to do is seek God. When we seek him, he will be found—and his perfect plans for us will begin to unfold. Be open to letting God stretch you and your abilities. Be willing to follow wherever you feel he is directing you. Remember, God knows your life better than you do, so let him take hold of it.

Running with a Purpose

Running has been a part of our family for years. Dad and Mom ran ten-kilometer races and a marathon when they were in college. Mom was also a track coach when she first started teaching school. I (Grace) run on the high-school cross-country team, and both of us have competed on the school track team. We've learned many life lessons through our track experiences—lessons on the importance of discipline, determination, perseverance, and most importantly, keeping our eyes on the finish line.

The writer of Hebrews likened our journey of life to a race. Here's what he said in Hebrews 12:1–2:

> Therefore, since we are surrounded by such a huge crowd of witnesses to the life of faith, let us strip off every weight that slows us down, especially the sin that so easily hinders our progress. And let us run with endurance the race that God has set before us. We do this by keeping our eyes on Jesus, on whom our faith depends from start to finish. He was willing to die a shameful death on the cross because of the joy he knew would be his afterward. Now he is seated in the place of highest honor beside God's throne in heaven.

According to this passage, we are all participants in the race of life. Our job is to keep our eyes on Jesus, run with endurance, and lay aside the heavy things that slow us down. As a family of long-distance runners, we have a very practical understanding of that last directive. In fact, during track season, I (Grace) often repeated Hebrews 12:1–2 in my head as I ran, and it encouraged me. Since any extra baggage could slow us down and keep us from winning a particular race, we've learned to be careful not to wear or carry anything that could encumber us.

What are those things that slow us down from our purpose and take our eyes off Jesus? Here are a few common weights that can steer us off course.

Material Things

No doubt about it, we live in a materialistic culture. Everywhere we go, we are bombarded with messages advertising things that we may not need but sure do want. It's easy to get caught up in our wants, letting them consume our time, energy, and money. The desire to have more can easily take our eyes off our goal of seeking God's best for us.

Take Jason, who was consumed with the desire for a Hummer sports utility vehicle. He loved these cars (or should we say, tanks) and wanted one with a passion. His parents agreed to help a little toward paying for a car, but the main burden for raising the money was on Jason. So he worked extra hours bagging groceries and cutting lawns on the side in order to pay for his dream. Every penny he made went to the car fund. For quite a while, he didn't have much of a life beyond work, school, athletics, eating, and sleeping.

Finally the time came when Jason had saved enough money, and he became the proud owner of a Hummer SUV. No one else at school had a car so grand and glorious. But while the car was paid for, the gas, insurance, and maintenance costs weren't. Jason had to work even harder and longer to take care of his prized vehicle. After several long months, he began to realize he had become a slave to his car. It guzzled gas, it needed repairs, and the newness factor of owning such a unique vehicle eventually wore off. So Jason sold the Hummer, bought an inexpensive car that got great gas mileage, and simplified his life.

Funny how the things we think we want the most can weigh us down, steal our joy, and rob us of precious time we could be using for something more productive! We all need to take continual inventory of the material things that paw for our attention—things like cars, electronics, CDs, expensive clothes, jewelry. Is it wrong to like nice things or have lots of stuff? Not necessarily. The question we must ask ourselves is, do these things dominate our hearts and lives? Do we give so much attention to material things that we have little time or desire to seek God's face? The love of material things can be idolatry in disguise.

The Comparison Trap

It's pretty common for us to look at certain teenagers and complain about how smart they are, how good-looking they are, or how popular they are, feeling as if we fall short in comparison. It's also common for us to look at other teenagers and think, *Well, I look better than her,* or, *I'm smarter than him.* One direction makes us feel awful about ourselves, opening the door to envy and jealousy. The other direction leads us to become prideful. Either direction can consume our minds and hearts and steer us off course, away from our life's purpose. We need to follow our own God-given course and be the best we can be.

Bad Relationships

There is an age-old principle that seems to always hold true: we become just like the company we keep. So be careful about the friends you hang around! Thinking, *I'm going to be a good influence on this person. I can handle it,* just isn't wise. As Paul warns, "Bad company corrupts good morals" (1 Corinthians 15:33). Rarely, if ever, do good companions help the bad ones become better people. It's OK to have *acquaintances* of all different types, but *companions* are a different story. We need to make sure that the close friends we chose are wise, God-fearing people.

We'll talk more about this later in the relationship section of the book. For now we just want to point out that bad company can have a negative impact on our lives. Close relationships with other teens who don't share our faith and values can be a big factor in throwing us off course in the race of life.

The steps of the godly are directed by the LORD. He delights in every detail of their lives. —Psalm 37:23

Pride

Falling is one of the worst things that can happen to a racer. It's discouraging, physically damaging, and can put a runner behind the pack. The Bible is clear that pride is one of those things that causes us to fall in our life race. It trips us up and keeps our eyes off the goal of serving Jesus. How? By causing us to put our eyes on ourselves. It's interesting that in the same chapter of Proverbs where we find the verse "Commit your work to the LORD, and then your plans will succeed" (Proverbs 16:3), we also find "The LORD despises pride; be assured that the proud will be punished" (v. 5) and "Pride goes before destruction, and haughtiness before a fall" (v. 18).

It's when we take our eyes off Christ and start thinking, *I can succeed in life on my own,* that we begin to stumble. How easy it is to get our eyes centered on ourselves! In one moment we can be thanking God for allowing us to make the cheerleading squad or the football team, and in the next moment we can begin thinking, *I'm so good. I deserved to make it!* We need to pray that the Lord keeps our vision clear. As the psalmist said, "Create in me a clean heart, O God, and renew a right spirit within me" (Psalm 51:10).

Continual Sin

Often we minimize or dismiss our sins, thinking they don't really affect us. But sin is the heaviest weight that loads us down in the race of life. Can you picture running a six-mile race with a backpack full of bricks? That's what we look like when we continually choose to do the things that we know are wrong. Yes, we all sin. Not one of us is perfect. Thank the Lord we are perfectly forgiven through Christ! But we do need to recognize sin for what it is and get it out of our lives, so we can run our race unhindered.

Even Christians can get caught up in devastating sin. If that happens to us, we need to admit our sin, get help if necessary, and ask someone we trust to hold us accountable for breaking the sin cycle. In Galatians 6, Christians are instructed to help others who have been caught in the sin trap: "Dear brothers and sisters, if another Christian is overcome by some sin, you who are godly should gently and humbly help that person back onto the right path" (v. 1).

Christina was definitely a Christian. She gave her life to Christ at an early age. But when she was sixteen, her boyfriend—a young man she thought she might marry—began pressing her to have sex. She finally gave in one lonely afternoon when her parents were away. It wasn't just a one-time affair; they began having sex at her house several times a week, before her parents got home from work. Soon Christina's focus was off of getting her education and following God's call of becoming a teacher. Instead, her thoughts were constantly about her boyfriend—and what her parents would do if they found out she was having sex. Christina didn't feel good about herself, and she certainly didn't want to pray to God about his plans for her life. How could she? She was so full of guilt and shame!

The truth is, God loves us no matter how we come to him. Through Christ he cleanses us and forgives us. But our life purpose can become clouded by sin. When we get caught up in doing wrong, it's easy to lose our bearings and forget that God loves us and has a wonderful plan for our lives.

In Christina's case, her plans completely changed when she became pregnant. No longer was she free to follow the plans she had hoped for; now her life was turned upside down. She decided to keep the baby, although her boyfriend soon moved out of the picture. Now Christina has a baby to raise, no college education, and no opportunities for the work she dreamed of doing. Certainly God can take the broken pieces of Christina's life—and our lives—and put them back together again.

But his perfect plan is for us to follow him and avoid the pain and suffering sin brings into our lives.

So What's the Plan?

Planning, planning—everything seems to come down to planning. Whether it's a plan to get together with friends on Saturday night or to study for a test, we all make plans; they help daily life to move along a little more smoothly.

But if our purpose is to honor God and we are seeking him to direct our paths, do we really need a big-picture plan for our lives? Good planning helps us move forward in the race of life in a positive way, allowing us to do the best with what God has given us. To be positive teens, we really do need a plan.

Most businesses create strategic plans for their organizations to help them achieve their goals. We've found that a little personal strategic planning is helpful to keep us on track too. There are four areas on this journey of life that demand our attention:

1. Physical

Are you taking care of yourself physically, so you can be the best you can be? God has a great purpose for each of our lives, and staying healthy allows us the freedom to carry it out. Eating right, exercising, and getting enough rest all play a part in our physical well-being. You may want to consider creating a plan for yourself that includes maintaining a healthy diet, keeping up a reasonable exercise routine, and creating a schedule to help you get the rest you need.

I (Joy) am rarely in the mood to work out, so a couple of friends and I decided to take kickboxing classes together. The classes have become a fun way to stay in shape—plus we are able to keep one another accountable!

2. Mental

What are you doing with your brain? Are you wasting it on video games or trash TV, or are you making the most of the intellect God has given you? Of course, there is a time for relaxing. But there is also a time for mental growth and stimulation. Consider setting a plan to achieve the grades you know you ought to be getting in school. How much time do you need to study? What amount of time can or should you devote to "vegging out" with mindless activities?

3. Social

Our relationships with others are important to God. Jesus was quite clear that he wants us to love each other. "I command you to love each other in the same way that I love you," he said in John 15:12. What this means is that we need to be deliberate about building positive relationships and showing love to the people around us. Consider making a plan to reach out to other teenagers. It might involve inviting people over, calling a friend, or even writing a note to someone who needs a lift.

Personally, I (Grace) try to maintain my current friendships and build new ones by getting involved in Bible studies, student leadership events, and organizations like Fellowship of Christian Athletes. I make a point of calling people and encouraging them to be a part of these activities. My participation in these groups has given me many opportunities to reach out to others.

4. Spiritual

We are not just our physical bodies; we are spiritual beings too. As such, we need to make sure that we're giving our spiritual selves the attention and nourishment we need. We will look more closely at spiritual growth in chapters 14 and 15. For now, consider making a plan for your life that includes regular time alone with God for prayer and studying his Word. You may even want to make a plan to memorize the scriptures we suggest in the Power Point section of each chapter.

Planning is a good, positive way to move forward in fulfilling our purpose in life. And that purpose is twofold. Our life purpose as Christians is to love God and honor him. Our personal purpose is more specific; it's between us and God as he moves us along the pathway of life. You may not know or understand God's entire plan for your life at this point. But that shouldn't keep you from making personal strategic plans as he reveals more and more of the road ahead of you.

God's Power in You

If you stay on the road God has planned for you, there's no limit to what he can do in you and through you! It's not prideful to look heavenward and realize that God can take simple vessels like us and do great and mighty things for his purpose. Throughout the Bible we see that God took the most unlikely people and worked great eternal purposes through them. Think of Moses, who stuttered; David, who was small; Daniel, who was a stranger and a captive; Peter, who was a bigmouthed, burly fisherman; or even the little boy who had only two fish and five loaves of bread. God had a plan for each of them, and God has a plan for each of us.

Don't worry that you don't have it all figured out! "'My thoughts are completely different from yours,' says the LORD. 'And my ways are far beyond anything you could imagine. For just as the heavens are higher than the earth, so are my ways higher than your ways and my thoughts higher than your thoughts'" (Isaiah 55:8–9). The God of the universe sees the whole picture; we only see what is in front of us. Why would we hesitate to seek him for direction?

God has a purpose for our existence. He has an eternal plan and a specific calling for each of us. What is our job? To plan and manipulate and scheme and drive? No. We *should* make strategic plans and set personal goals as God reveals his will to us, but our main job is to seek—to seek Christ and keep our eyes on him. As we do, he will direct our paths to places we could never dream or imagine. And we'll become positive teens along the way.

POWER POINT

Read: 1 Samuel 17:12–58. Where were the Israelites' eyes directed? Where did David have his eyes pointed? What negative influences did David face in this passage? How would you describe David's faith?

Pray: Perfect Lord and Savior, your plans are perfect, and your ways are perfect. My plans are simple: I place my trust in you. Please direct my path and lead me in the direction you want me to go. Help me to get rid of the weights that slow me down, throw me off course, and keep me from following you. Show me the weights I don't even see right now, and give me the strength to lay them aside. Bring someone into my life who is spiritually mature, who can help me and hold me accountable in the areas where I struggle. Most importantly, shine your love through me, and help me to be a useful and willing vessel for your eternal purpose. In Jesus's name, amen.

Remember: Psalm 37:23: "The steps of the godly are directed by the LORD. He delights in every detail of their lives."

Do: Take a moment and ask God to create a clean heart and renew a right spirit in you. Ask him to lead you along the path he has planned for you and keep you from getting caught up in your own sin or distractions. Write out your commitment to keep your eyes on him on an index or note card, and place the card in your Bible. Remind yourself of your commitment each time you open God's Word.

Power Principle #2

THe Power oF ResPonSIbility

*He has showed you, O man, what is good.
And what does the LORD require of you? To act justly and to love mercy
and to walk humbly with your God.*

—Micah 6:8 NIV

No man can always be right. So the struggle is to do one's best; to keep the brain and conscience clear; never to be swayed by unworthy motives or inconsequential reasons, but to strive to unearth the basic factors involved and then do one's duty.

—Dwight D. Eisenhower

Success 101
Earning Respect at Work and in Life

Work hard and cheerfully at whatever you do, as though you were working for the Lord rather than for people.

—Colossians 3:23

One of our favorite Aesop's fables goes like this:

> One fine day in winter some ants were busy drying their store of corn, which had got rather damp during a long spell of rain. Presently up came a grasshopper and begged them to spare her a few grains. "For," she said, "I'm simply starving." The ants stopped work for a moment, though this was against their principles.
>
> "May we ask," said they, "what you were doing with yourself all last summer? Why didn't you collect a store of food for the winter?"
>
> "The fact is," replied the grasshopper, "I was so busy singing that I hadn't the time."
>
> "If you spent the summer singing," replied the ants, "you can't do better than spend the winter dancing." And they chuckled and went on with their work.[1]

The ant seems like an unlikely source to teach us about success in life, but Solomon didn't think so. Just as Aesop's fable reflects the wisdom of the ant's diligent work, so does the book of Proverbs. Take a look at the lessons from the ant directed to a person called "lazybones" in Proverbs 6:6–11:

> Take a lesson from the ants, you lazybones. Learn from their ways and be wise! Even though they have no prince, governor, or ruler to make them work, they labor hard all summer, gathering food for the winter. But you, lazybones, how long will you sleep? When will you wake up? I want you to learn this lesson: A little extra sleep, a little more slumber, a little folding of the hands to rest—and poverty will pounce on you like a bandit; scarcity will attack you like an armed robber.

Later in Proverbs 30:25 we read, "There are four things on earth that are small but unusually wise: Ants—they aren't strong, but they store up food for the winter." (Check out the verse for the other three things.) We don't need to be stronger or bigger or even more intelligent than other people in order to be wise and successful in life. No, success comes down to one quality: being responsible in our work.

Maybe you're saying to yourself, *I'm just a teenager. I don't have to think about the working world yet.* The truth is, all of us work in some way or another, whether it's doing homework, finishing chores, babysitting, or having a part-time job. The valuable lessons we can learn from the ant will help us now, and they will last for a lifetime. Laziness only leads to boredom and an unproductive life, whether we're sixteen or sixty. Often it can get us into trouble and lead to unfortunate consequences, as it did for Aesop's grasshopper.

Work is a part of life that we can either embrace and value or abhor and avoid. But it won't go away. The question is, what will our attitude be toward work?

For the Love of Work

Through responsibility and work, we can experience both fulfillment and joy. It's true! A vocation can actually energize us and give us purpose and meaning. On the other hand, laziness and boredom can drain us of excitement and energy. When we sit around doing nothing of value, our strength is zapped, not renewed. Why? Because we were created to be working beings. From the very beginning in the Garden of Eden, Adam and Eve were given the responsibility to "tend and care" for the garden (Genesis 2:15).

God continues to call us to responsible work in the New Testament: "Work hard and cheerfully at whatever you do, as though you were working for the Lord rather than for people. Remember that the Lord will give you an inheritance as your reward, and the Master you are serving is Christ" (Colossians 3:23–24). What a wonderful encouragement! We are not simply working for an earthly reward, but we are serving the Lord Jesus. He's the one who sees our every deed and rewards us eternally for our responsible actions. How motivating!

So whether our work is homework, housework, or full-time, make-a-living work, we need to embrace it. You may be wondering, *Is it really possible to work cheerfully in any job?* Well, in terms of our future life's work, we'll definitely have an easier time of it if we find a career that suits us. We'll talk about that more in a minute. But even if we have no choice about our work—for example, when we have to do chores or homework—we can learn to find the "cheer" in it.

Say you have to study for a history test. You may not like history; you may even detest it. But you can take a positive approach by accepting the task, refusing to grumble about it, and looking for a way to make it more interesting. You could picture yourself living in the time

57

period you're studying, for example, and then think about how you would have handled the issues of that day. (Try it; it works!)

Bottom line, we don't have to completely love studying history or anything else that we do; we just have to approach our work with acceptance, cheer, and responsibility instead of grumbling, griping, and laziness. When we do that, we're on the right road to becoming positive teens. Now don't get us wrong—we both struggle with having a good attitude toward work; we're not saying it is easy. We're saying it is right.

Wonderful Work

Of course, most of us will have a job—most likely, many jobs—in our lifetimes. It may be part-time now and full-time later. Either way, working in a job is not something to be dreaded but rather something to be honored.

Granted, all jobs aren't always fun. Some can get downright boring. But when we find ourselves using and developing the gifts God has given us in a particular job, we can find great pleasure in doing what we have to do.

Often when people dread or dislike work, it's because they're in the wrong job, misusing their gifts, talents, and abilities. That doesn't mean that we shouldn't work until we find the perfect job that plays only to our strengths. There is no perfect job! We repeat: there is no perfect job, either now or in the future, that will serve our interests, talents, and abilities exactly to a tee. Even a job that seems to be a good fit will stretch us in certain areas. Every job has its joys as well as its challenges. We shouldn't wait until the right work comes along; we have to find good work, and make it right for us! As B. C. Forbes says, "Whether we find pleasure in work or whether we find it a bore depends entirely on our mental attitude."[2]

When we do more than we are paid to do, eventually we will be paid more for what we do. —Zig Ziglar

Bottom line, the secret to success in any job is not doing what we like, but rather liking what we do. Will Rogers put it this way: "In order to succeed, you must know what you are doing, like what you are doing, and believe in what you are doing."[3] Think about it. As we take on a new job, we must first understand what we're doing and what's expected of us. Just because we find a job that utilizes our talents doesn't mean we can coast and boast. We can't sit back and think we know it all. We need to be continually learning.

Second, we must like what we are doing. Again, that doesn't mean we should shop around until we find the perfect job that makes us perfectly happy. It means we should find a job that we believe we are competent to do and then find something we like within it.

Finally, according to Will Rogers, we must believe in what we're doing. Last summer I (Grace) worked at Nordstrom's department store. Nordstrom's, I discovered, is devoted in every way to serving their customers and offers its employees extensive customer service training. I was proud to work for such an upstanding company, which has built its reputation on quality and service. And because I believed in the organization, I found myself wanting to represent it well. I tried to keep in mind what we learned from Colossians: my ultimate boss is the Lord. I wanted to represent him well most of all.

Working Responsibly

There are certain principles every person should follow when it comes to working for another person. As teenagers, we really need to understand these principles and start putting them into practice now. Our commitment to these principles will eventually take us beyond being entry-level workers to becoming successful employees moving ahead in the company—and successful people moving ahead in life. These principles may seem simple or obvious, but they're absolutely critical to being a success. All of them have a scriptural basis that we encourage you to look up.

1. Show up on time—be early; don't find excuses to be late (Proverbs 26:13).

2. Have a great attitude; show enthusiasm (Philippians 4:4).

3. Ask for assistance if you don't understand what you are supposed to do (Proverbs 4:7).

4. Serve—serve the customer, serve the boss, serve the company (Mark 10:43).

5. Never gossip or slander a fellow employee (Proverbs 30:10).

6. Never complain; do all things without grumbling (Philippians 2:14).

7. Be patient with all people (Colossians 3:12).

8. Be honest in everything you do and say (Psalm 37:37).

9. Do more than you are asked to do; exceed expectations instead of barely meeting them (Colossians 3:23, Proverbs 27:18).

OK, OK—we realize it may sound as if we expect everyone to be perfect on the job. Our intention is not to throw you or anyone else onto a perfectionist performance track. None of us are perfect workers—especially teenagers. We're new at this job stuff! But we *can* strive to be as responsible as we can possibly be. Look at the following poem by Edgar Guest. It speaks to the glory and reward of doing our work to the best of our ability:

True Nobility

Who does his task from day to day
And meets whatever comes his way,
Believing God has willed it so,

Has found real greatness here below.

Who guards his post, no matter where,

Believing God must need him there,

Although but lowly toil it be,

Has risen to nobility.

For great and low there's but one test:

'Tis that each man shall do his best.

Who works with all the strength he can

Shall never die in debt to man.[4]

Maybe you're thinking, *But what if I make a mistake? What if I'm trying my best at my job, and I mess up?* That's bound to happen to all of us—not because we're teenagers, but because we're human. It can happen at any time in our lives or careers. What is the most positive way to respond? There are four steps:

1. Acknowledge your mistake. Own up to it and take responsibility for your actions. Don't blame someone else for something that's your fault.

2. Apologize. Go to your superiors, your co-workers, the customers, or whoever is involved, and make a full and sincere apology for your actions.

3. Correct the situation. Do everything in your power to make things right.

4. Move on. Don't wallow in regret, keep apologizing, or tell yourself you're a failure. Simply commit yourself to doing better next time.

When Is a Job Not Right for You?

Sometimes when a job is a "bad fit," the most positive thing to do is to find a different job. We're not talking about running away from a job because it's stretching or challenging us. There is a fine line between sticking to a job even when it gets challenging and knowing when to change jobs because we're in a bad situation. Commitment is an important character quality that we should nurture and develop. If at all possible, we ought to carry out whatever it is that we have committed to do. But there are valid reasons for leaving a job. Here are a few examples:

- If your employer is abusive in any way
- If your boss blames you for his or her mistakes or takes credit for your accomplishments
- If you are in a job that is not a good fit for your gifts and talents, and another job opportunity becomes available
- If your employer is dishonest or asks you to be dishonest

Take Mary, who got a summer job working at a local sporting goods store. At first she enjoyed her job; she seemed to have a real gift for working with people. But then the big summer sales event came around. Mary's boss told her that she should intentionally "forget" the advertised discount unless the customer brought it up. She should charge full price and hope the customer didn't notice.

Mary knew she was being asked to do something deceptive, and she felt wrong about it in her spirit. When she approached the manager about her concern, he laughed it off and told her, "Stop being such a goody-goody." Soon she began to notice several other dishonest and underhanded policies being practiced at the store. So even though she'd told the manager that she would work there all summer, she decided to quit. She realized this store was not the place for her.

Maybe you're in a job right now that you think you want to quit. We can't tell you what to do, since we don't know all the circumstances. We do recommend, however, that you be honest with yourself and evaluate your decision carefully. Talk it through with your parents or a trusted friend who can help you see your situation clearly. Breaking a commitment is serious business. It's not something to do because the job is "not fun anymore" or tougher than you thought it would be.

Consider Steve, who accepted a job as a pet sitter while a family in his neighborhood went on vacation for two weeks. When the neighbors first talked to him about taking the job, they told him that all he would need to do was feed the dogs twice a day and let them out in the backyard for a while. When he arrived at the house on the first day of his commitment, however, he found a note informing him that he also needed to "scoop the poop" in the backyard. *What? I don't even like these dogs, and now I have to clean up their poop?* Steve thought angrily. *This is not what I agreed to do!*

Steve did his job that day, but he went home seething and threatening to quit. The next morning, he got up early so he could go back to his neighbors' house. Before he left, however, he decided to pray that God would show him the attitude he ought to have. He remembered Joseph in the pit and serving in prison. He thought about Jesus washing the disciples' dirty feet. Didn't Christ come to serve, not to be served? He began to realize that although his job was not what he thought he'd signed up for and had some less-than-enjoyable aspects, he was committed to doing it. His neighbors were depending upon him. So Steve stuck to the job and leaned on God's power and strength to help him keep his commitment with a positive attitude.

Don't Make Excuses!

Proverbs 22:13 says, "The lazy person is full of excuses, saying, 'If I go outside, I might meet a lion in the street and be killed.'" What are some of the excuses that come out of our mouths when we want to avoid work?

- "I don't feel good."
- "If I clean it now, it will just get dirty all over again."
- "I overslept."
- "I forgot my math book."

Excuses are easy to make. Sometimes they're even based on truth. But if we're brutally honest, we have to admit that we often lean on the

Hard workers have plenty of food; playing around brings poverty. —Proverbs 28:19

excuses to cover up our own laziness or irresponsibility. Paul came down pretty hard on some excuse-makers in the early church. The Christians in Thessalonica were very excited about Christ's second coming. Perhaps they were a little too fired up, because many of them decided to stop working and simply wait for Christ's return.

Unfortunately, laziness and idleness can lead to meddling and gossip. That's what was happening in Thessalonica. So Paul wrote this stern rebuke:

> And now, dear brothers and sisters, we give you this command with the authority of our Lord Jesus Christ: Stay away from any Christian who lies in idleness and doesn't follow the tradition of hard work we gave you. For you know that you ought to follow our example. We were never lazy when we were with you. We never accepted food from anyone without paying for it. We worked hard day and night so that we would not be a burden to any of you. It wasn't that we didn't have the right to ask you to feed us, but we wanted to give you an example to follow. Even while we were with you, we gave you this rule: "Whoever does not work should not eat."
>
> Yet we hear that some of you are living idle lives, refusing to work and wasting time meddling in other people's business. In the name of the Lord Jesus Christ, we appeal to such people—no, we command them: settle down and get to work. Earn your own living. And I say to the rest of you, dear brothers and sisters, never get tired of doing good. (2 Thessalonians 3:6–13)

Paul didn't leave too much to guesswork here! The Christians in Thessalonica were basing their laziness on the truth that Jesus would return. As we said, most excuses are built on some truth. Here's another truth: we all need time to relax and chill out. Relaxation provides a necessary balance in life. Our loving heavenly Father even provided a day of rest, knowing that we all need to cease from our labors at least one day each week. But we can't confuse leisure with laziness. We need to make sure we work when we ought to be working and rest when we ought to be resting. Yes, we need to relax. We just don't need to relax all the time!

If we are going to be real with others and with ourselves, then we must not hide behind truth and use it as an excuse for laziness and irresponsibility. Paul was quite clear that being lazy and idle only leads to trouble. So was Solomon in the book of Proverbs. Proverbs 18:9 reminds us, "A lazy person is as bad as someone who destroys things." And Proverbs 21:25 says, "The desires of lazy people will be their ruin, for their hands refuse to work." Not only is work good for us, but laziness and excuses are bad for us!

Benjamin Franklin was a colorful, resourceful inventor and statesman—and he was anything but lazy. He wrote this little jingle as a warning against excuses:

Mr. Meant-To

Mr. Meant-To has a comrade,
And his name is Didn't-Do;
Have you ever chanced to meet them?
Did they ever call on you?
These two fellows live together
In the house of Never-Win,
And I'm told that it is haunted
By the ghost of Might-Have-Been.[5]

We can't be positive teens until we shed the excuses, embrace our work, and learn to find joy in the midst of any job we're called to do. Today that may involve school assignments, baby-sitting, flipping hamburgers, or helping around the house. In a few years, it may involve full-time employment in the marketplace. Whatever our work is, both now and later, let's work hard, cheerfully, and responsibly. That's the positive thing to do. After all, we're not just working for an A in history, a paycheck, an allowance, or a pat on the back. We're working for the Lord. Let's make our work an act of worship, giving our all to Christ.

POWER POINT

⚙ **Read:** 1 Thessalonians 5:12–23. Underline every phrase that is good advice for being responsible in your work. How does this passage encourage you to approach your own responsibilities? What do you think you need to work on? Why is it important for Christians to do a good job?

◉ **Pray:** Dear wonderful heavenly Father, thank you for being my Lord and my leader. It is so wonderful to know that I ultimately work for you. You are my reward! You see the good work I do, even if no one else notices it. Thank you for the gifts, talents, and abilities you have given me that allow me to carry out the work you have planned for my life. Thank you for the strength and power you offer me each day through your Holy Spirit. Help me to be responsible in my work. Help me to do the very best job I can do in order to represent you well. In Jesus's name I pray, amen.

♡ **Remember:** Proverbs 21:5: "Good planning and hard work lead to prosperity, but hasty shortcuts lead to poverty."

☺ **Do:** Take a moment for self-evaluation using the list of nine principles for success found on page 60. Are there any areas you need to work on in order to become a more responsible student, worker, or employee? What do you see as your primary jobs at this time in your life, and what is your attitude toward them? What can you do to make better use of idle (not leisure) time? Do you have any ideas for starting a business, getting a job, or working around the house? Ask the Lord to lead you in using the gifts he has given you.

Who Wants to Be a Millionaire?
Managing Your Money

Trust in your money and down you go! But the godly
flourish like leaves in spring.

—Proverbs 11:28

I t was a Sunday morning to remember, to say the least. As we sat in the pew, we were each handed an envelope with the words *Do not open until instructed* written on the front. The preacher gave an inspiring message about investing in eternal things rather than in things that will fade away. Then he instructed us to open our envelopes.

We admit our first thought was that the envelope would contain another envelope asking us to give money to the church. To our surprise it was quite the opposite. Inside every envelope was one ten-dollar bill and one five-dollar bill. As we looked around, we saw that everyone was drawing out the same amount from their envelopes, along with a note that read:

An Investment Strategy

Since God owns it all, the money in this envelope is given to you to help someone in need. You may use it any way you want except:

1. Please don't put the money in the church offering box.
2. Please don't spend it on yourself.

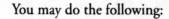

You may do the following:

1. Use the money to meet a need outside the church body.
2. Combine your money with another person's money.
3. Pool your money together as a group.
4. Add this money with other funds to increase the amount given.[1]

The fact that our church didn't have a large, overflowing budget made this challenge all the more extraordinary. Our pastor encouraged us to be creative, pray, and let God lead us as to how to use the money. Our thoughts began to race as we pondered the best way to share our fifteen dollars with someone in need.

Mom wanted to combine our money and use it to buy Bibles to hand out to people. Dad wanted to use the combined sum to buy food to feed the homeless. We finally decided on a compromise: we would use some of the money for food and some for Bibles, and we would hand out the food and Bibles together. With great joy we joined several other church members and journeyed to downtown Dallas to feed the homeless. It was a meaningful experience for us all. As we looked into the faces of the people we were serving and offered them food, a Bible, and a smile, we knew our money was being invested wisely.

Money can be used to bless people, but it can also be a curse in our lives. All too easily, it can end up consuming our thoughts, desires, time, and interests. The Bible actually talks quite a bit about money. There are about five hundred verses in the Bible on prayer and less than five hundred on faith, but there are two thousand verses on the issue of money and possessions.[2] Of the thirty-eight parables Jesus told, sixteen were about the handling of money and material things. Obviously, money matters! The challenge for each of us is to maintain a right

God entrusts us with money as a test; for like a toy to the child, it is training for handling things of more value. —Fred Smith

perspective concerning money and learn how to use it wisely. The teenage years are a good place to start.

Secret to Success

OK, let's say you have a wad of money in your hand—say, seventy-five dollars. Maybe you worked for it; maybe it was a gift; but it's yours to spend! So what are you going to do with it? Well, there's that leather jacket you've been wanting since last Christmas. There's also the cell phone you'd like to have. Maybe you could put it toward a new sound system or perhaps a stack of your favorite CDs. There are so many possibilities. It's a tough decision!

How do you decide what to do with your money? Teenagers are notorious for spending their money the moment they have it. Some of us are more miserly and rarely spend a dime. Neither extreme is particularly positive.

If we want our money to serve us well, then we need to have a plan for using it wisely. Most financial counselors recommend a tried-and-true method of handling income that leads to financial stability in the future as well as smart (yet enjoyable) spending in the present. It begins with setting aside 10 percent of the money we receive and placing it directly into savings. It is never too early to open a savings account. This money can be set aside for a designated future use—perhaps purchasing a car or having spending money in college. Then, as we get older and have a more regular income, we can systematically deposit a portion of our money into an additional savings account for emergencies.

As Christians we know that the Bible encourages us to set aside 10 percent of our income to give to the Lord. That 10 percent is called a tithe. We see the first tithe in the Bible offered by Abram (later called Abraham) after he had returned from a victorious battle to rescue his nephew Lot. In Genesis 14:20 we read, "Then Abram gave

Melchizedek a tenth of all the goods he had recovered." The concept of tithing (which was an offering to God) again appears in Deuteronomy 26:12, as God instructs the Israelites, "Every third year you must offer a special tithe of your crops. You must give these tithes to the Levites, foreigners, orphans, and widows so that they will have enough to eat in your towns." Later in Nehemiah 10:37, the Israelites say, "And we promise to bring to the Levites a tenth of everything our land produces, for it is the Levites who collect the tithes in all our rural towns." Of course, giving to the church and to those in need does not need to be limited to 10 percent of our income, but the tithe gives us a place to start.

Form the habit of tithing now! As we get older and our paychecks increase, giving may become more difficult. You might think it would be the other way around, but consider this: if you make one hundred dollars, giving ten dollars doesn't seem like a big deal. But if you make ten thousand dollars, your tithe is one thousand dollars, and that may seem like a bigger sacrifice. If you make five hundred thousand dollars, then fifty thousand dollars may seem like a huge chunk to give away! If we stay faithful in the small giving now, the large giving later will come a little more naturally. Ultimately, giving is a heart issue. As God moves in our hearts with compassion toward others and creates an attitude of gratitude within us, we will become givers—and positive teens to boot. We just need to ask God to help us develop open hearts and open hands.

Budgeting for Wants versus Needs

Let's say you have saved your 10 percent and given your 10 percent to God. That leaves you with a whopping 80 percent to spend! The question is, what are you going to do with it? The most positive, prudent thing would be to spend your money on your needs first and then on your wants—not the other way around. We know that may sound obvious, but we also know (from experience) how easy it is to let the gas money we need to get to school slip through our hands to buy a cute shirt or a hamburger at the drive-thru. It's so easy to spend frivolously and then end up with no money to spend on what we really need! As one mother of teenagers told us when she found out we were writing this chapter, "It's not in spending money that teenagers need help; it's in saving it. They are already experts in spending it."

That's why we need to learn now, as teenagers, how to make every spending decision a wise decision. Before we let money flow out of our hands and over the counter, we need to think, *Is this something I really need to spend my money on right now, or is there something more important that I need to save it for?*

Take a moment right now to think about the things you need to spend money on each month. Maybe your parents give you a certain amount in allowance, or you have to earn your own money to pay for gas, clothing, lunch at school, or movies on the weekend. Maybe you are in the midst of paying back your parents for a broken window or speeding ticket or dent in the car. Whatever your circumstances, make a list of the things you need to spend money on monthly, along with the approximate dollar amount. We'll even give you a little space right here to do it:

My Need	Dollar Amount
1. _____	_____
2. _____	_____
3. _____	_____
4. _____	_____
5. _____	_____

Now add up the total dollar amount and add a little cushion (since most of us tend to underestimate expenses). This total is what you need to set aside and protect against "but I want it" spending. Whatever you have left over is the amount you can spend on wants.

Of course, this will never work for any of us if we don't take the time and make the effort to discern between our wants and our needs. Distinguishing between wants and needs is possibly the single most important financial principle we can learn. Making this distinction will not only help us to be money-wise as teenagers; it will help us to be financially sound and secure throughout our lives. It takes self-control and discipline to use our money for the essentials first and our desires later, but it's worth the effort. As Proverbs 10:16 says, "The earnings of the godly enhance their lives, but evil people squander their money on sin."

Believe it or not, a lot of good comes from having to wait to fulfill our desires. We become patient and wise. We learn to be content with what we have until we can have what we want. Contentment is an important attribute for positive teens—and for Christians in general. Amazingly, Paul wrote these words about contentment while he was in a prison cell: "I have learned to be content whatever the circumstances. I know what it is to be in need, and I know what it is to have plenty. I have learned the secret of being content in any and every situation, whether well fed or hungry, whether living in plenty or in want. I can do everything through him who gives me strength" (Philippians 4:11–13 NIV).

Perhaps you've heard the phrase "I can do everything through Christ." But you may not have realized that Paul was using those words to describe his key to being content. Contentment is a rare commodity in today's gotta-have-more society. It takes God's patience and strength to be content with what we have and not continually crave more. Contentment isn't laziness, and it's not giving up. It's simply saying, "If I can't buy what I want right now, I'll be OK with that. God will give me the strength to wait until I can afford it." The key is taking care of your needs before your wants—and having the discernment to know the difference.

Debt or No Debt

We live in a debt-happy society. Many people have grown too comfortable with debt, which only leads to financial instability. Most wise financial advisers caution against going into debt, except for the purchase of a house and possibly a car. The problem is, credit cards are so easily available; people charge all of their wants and needs to their credit cards, then pay the minimum payment each month instead of paying off the balance. Their debt builds up with a huge interest rate and often becomes a mountain of money that must be paid back to the creditor over many years.

What does this have to do with us as teenagers? Well, some of us have access to our parents' credit cards, or we think that because our parents have credit cards, nothing we want should be out of reach. And credit card companies are notorious for sending "free" credit cards or applications to new college students or other older teens, hoping to pull them into the debt trap at an early age.

A good idea is to only use a credit card as a matter of convenience and then to always (and we mean *always*) pay it off each month. Otherwise, you end up losing your financial freedom. Consider Kelsey's situation. When she first went off to college, she responded to a letter in the mail that offered her a shiny new credit card of her very own. She quickly realized how easy it was to buy everything with the card (clothes, makeup, groceries, movies, and so on). Even better, she only had to pay a small minimum balance each month! Whenever she handed that little credit card over the counter, it hardly seemed as if she was spending at all. The problem was, the low interest rate that the letter promised in the beginning was raised to 16 percent a few months later. Before she knew it, Kelsey had accumulated twenty thousand dollars of debt, with $3,200 in interest alone!

The real measure of our wealth is how much we'd be worth if we lost all our money. —John Henry Jowett

Now, if we were to say, "If you give us $3,200, we'll delay your debt payment. Of course, your debt will keep increasing in the meantime," you would say, "You're crazy!" But that's exactly what people like Kelsey do every month.

So when you receive that letter in the mail that says you have been preapproved for a credit card, tear it up! Don't take on a credit card until you are ready to have the responsibility of paying it off each month. There are times when you need a credit card—for example, when you're renting a car or checking into a hotel or buying something on the Internet. Credit cards, if used properly, can be used to establish a good financial history and credit rating for future purchases, such as a house. The key is to use your credit card; don't let your credit card use you!

Here's one more reason to stay out of debt as a teenager and young adult. Do you intend to get married one day? Racking up a debt of forty thousand dollars may be a real deal-killer for any potential spouse. Who wants to marry someone and immediately be in major debt? No matter how cute you are, being debt-free is a lot more appealing!

Don't create a monster through credit card spending. Debt is only a troublemaker, never a problem solver.

Principles from Proverbs

As we said earlier, money is mentioned in the Bible more times than even faith or prayer. One book in particular that talks a lot about money management is Proverbs. Warning: you may or may not enjoy reading every one of these principles, but they are wisdom for life nonetheless.

On Generosity

- Proverbs 11:24–25: "It is possible to give freely and become more wealthy, but those who are stingy will lose everything. The generous prosper and are satisfied; those who refresh others will themselves be refreshed."

- Proverbs 19:17: "If you help the poor, you are lending to the LORD—and he will repay you!"
- Proverbs 21:13: "Those who shut their ears to the cries of the poor will be ignored in their own time of need."
- Proverbs 22:9: "Blessed are those who are generous, because they feed the poor."

On Making Loans

- Proverbs 11:15: "Guaranteeing a loan for a stranger is dangerous; it is better to refuse than to suffer later."
- Proverbs 17:18: "It is poor judgment to co-sign a friend's note, to become responsible for a neighbor's debts."
- Proverbs 22:26–27: "Do not co-sign another person's note or put up a guarantee for someone else's loan. If you can't pay it, even your bed will be snatched from under you."

On Borrowing

- Proverbs 22:7: "Just as the rich rule the poor, so the borrower is servant to the lender."

On Saving for the Future

- Proverbs 21:20: "The wise have wealth and luxury, but fools spend whatever they get."

Understand, the Bible doesn't say that it's wrong to be rich, but it is wrong to love money and make it the center of our lives. God used many wealthy people to carry out his kingdom work throughout history, and he still does today. From Abraham to Joseph of Arimathea to Nicodemus, wealth has been a blessing to and through God's people.

The questions we have to ask ourselves are these: What am I really living for? Is my heart focused on having more money so I can accumulate more things? Or is my heart filled with contentment because it is centered on eternal things?

In Matthew 6 we read Jesus's words to his followers as he spoke what is now known as the Sermon on the Mount:

> Don't store up treasures here on earth, where they can be eaten by moths and get rusty, and where thieves break in and steal. Store your treasures in heaven, where they will never become moth-eaten or rusty and where they will be safe from thieves. Wherever your treasure is, there your heart and thoughts will also be. . . .
>
> No one can serve two masters. For you will hate one and love the other, or be devoted to one and despise the other. You cannot serve both God and money. (Matthew 6:19–21, 24)

The bottom line is this: guard your heart! It's so easy for us as teenagers to become enamored by the things of this world and all the pleasures that money can bring. It's not wrong to have money or to make money. We just can't let it dominate our hearts! The truth is, only as we find our contentment and happiness outside of money can we truly enjoy the money we have. Otherwise, our money rules over us, because we spend all of our time and energy worrying about how to get it and how to keep it.

Even Oprah Winfrey, one of the richest women in the world, claims to have found contentment outside of her wealth. "Before I had a lot of money, I was really quite happy," she once said. "And I will tell you this—you may not believe it—I never would have gotten the money if I wasn't happy to begin with. I never would have gotten it."[3]

John Rogers and Peter McWilliams, authors of *Wealth 101*, write that "wealth is enjoying what we already have, not getting more of what we think will make us happy."[4] To be positive teens, we need to start enjoying what we already have: a relationship with a God who loves us with a generous, grace-filled, everlasting love. We can't buy God's peace, joy, or contentment; they only come as we find our soul's satisfaction and our heart's desire in Christ alone. All the rest is fluff.

POWER POINT

Read: 1 Timothy 6:6–21. What instructions does Paul give to Timothy and the early Christians concerning money in this passage? Write down three lessons you can apply to your life.

Pray: Oh great Provider, you are all-sufficient! I know my deepest needs are met in you. Thank you for watching over me and taking care of me. I am richly blessed spiritually, materially, emotionally, and physically, because you are the One who meets my needs. May the love of money never creep into my heart and overtake my love for you and for others. Help me to be wise and discerning with what you have given me. Show me where and how to give of the resources you have put in my care. Thank you for your abundant love and grace, which are the greatest treasures of all. In Jesus's name I pray, amen.

Remember: Matthew 6:21: "Wherever your treasure is, there your heart and thoughts will also be."

Do: Take a critical look at your own spending habits. Are you being responsible to save and give properly? Are there any changes you need to make in the way you spend your money? Make a commitment to live within your means and be responsible with the resources God has entrusted to you.

Power Principle #3

THe Power oF InTeGriTy

Integrity is the basis of all true-blue success.

—B. C. Forbes

Praise the LORD! . . . Happy are those who delight in doing what he commands. Their children will be successful everywhere; an entire generation of godly people will be blessed. They themselves will be wealthy, and their good deeds will never be forgotten.

—Psalm 112:1–3

7

Living It Out
Developing Inward Character
That Affects Outward Actions

Create in me a clean heart, O God. Renew a right spirit within me.
—Psalm 51:10

The story is told of the famous nineteenth-century French artist Paul Gustave Doré, who was traveling between countries in Europe. As he came to a certain border, the immigration officer asked to see his passport. Doré searched his belongings then reported, "I have lost my passport, but it is all right. I'm Doré, the artist. Please let me go in."

The officer sternly replied, "Oh, no. We have plenty of people representing themselves as this or that great person! Here is a pencil and paper. Now, if you are Doré, the artist, prove it by drawing me a picture!"

Doré accepted the challenge, took the pencil, and drew pictures of scenes in the immediate area.

"Now, I am perfectly sure that you are Doré. No one else could draw like that!" said the officer, and he allowed the artist to enter the country.[1]

As this story illustrates, our actions reveal our true hearts; they show who we really are. The question is, what do *your* actions reveal? Do you have evidence to show that you are who you say you are? You may say that you are a Christian—a follower of Christ—but do your actions and words reveal that commitment? Or as someone has said, if you were on trial for being a Christian, would there be enough evidence to convict you?

It's easy to say we are Christians, but reflecting the title through our words and actions is another story. How are we living it out? Can other people see Jesus in us?

Portrait of Integrity

According to *Webster's Dictionary*, integrity is "the quality or state of being of sound moral principle; uprightness, honesty, and sincerity."[2] David Jeremiah describes integrity this way: "Integrity is keeping my commitment even if the circumstances when I made the commitment have changed."[3]

Personally, when we think of integrity, we think of a person whose actions and words reflect a heart that is committed to doing what is right in every circumstance. A person of integrity is a person with conviction—a conviction to be honest and genuine through and through. Most teenagers expect everyone from parents to politicians to be authentic. We're quick to come down on people (especially adults) who aren't "real." But can we turn that same criteria on ourselves and say, "I, too, am the real deal"?

Take Mark, for instance. He serves on the student council at school and is respected as a leader in sports and other activities. One day, in his hurry to get out of the school parking lot, he backs into another student's car. Now comes the moment of truth: will he leave a note on the other car to let the victim know who hit it, or will he drive off? No one was around to see the accident. No one would ever know. But because his integrity is important to him, Mark writes the note and sticks it under the other car's windshield wiper.

What about us? Can people trust our words and actions to be in line with who we say we are, even when no one is looking? Consider

Integrity is the integration of one's life around his core values. —William D. Lawrence

this poignant poem by Elizabeth Turner about a little girl with integrity:

Rebecca's Afterthought

Yesterday, Rebecca Mason,

In the parlor by herself,

Broke a handsome china basin

Placed upon the mantel shelf.

Quite alarmed, she thought of going

Very quietly away,

Not a single person knowing,

Of her being there that day.

But Rebecca recollected

She was taught deceit to shun;

And the moment she reflected,

Told her mother what was done;

Who commended her behavior,

Loved her better, and forgave her.[4]

That's the essence of integrity—doing what's right even when no one is watching us. And the truth is, there is someone who is always watching us—God. Proverbs 15:3 says, "The LORD is watching everywhere, keeping his eye on both the evil and the good." Another verse in Proverbs says that the "fear of the LORD is the beginning of knowledge" (1:7). A healthy fear of the Lord is a good thing. When we know that God is watching us and that he sees everything, we are motivated to live, walk, and talk with integrity. The following folk tale reminds us of this truth:

Once upon a time a man decided to sneak into his neighbor's fields and steal some wheat. "If I take just a little from each field, no one will notice," he told himself, "but it will all add up to a nice pile of wheat for me." So he waited for the darkest night, when thick clouds lay over the moon, and he crept out of his house. He took his youngest daughter with him.

"Daughter," he whispered, "you must stand guard, and call out if anyone sees me."

The man stole into the first field to begin reaping, and before long the child called out, "Father, someone sees you!"

The man looked all around, but he saw no one, so he gathered his stolen wheat and moved on to a second field.

"Father, someone sees you!" the child cried again.

The man stopped and looked all around, but once again he saw no one. He gathered more wheat, and moved to a third field.

A little while passed, and the daughter cried out, "Father, someone sees you!"

Once more the man stopped his work and looked in every direction, but he saw no one at all, so he bundled his wheat and crept into the last field.

"Father, someone sees you!" the child called again.

The man stopped his reaping, looked all around, and once again saw no one. "Why in the world do you keep saying someone sees me?" he angrily asked his daughter. "I've looked everywhere, and I don't see anyone."

"Father," murmured the child, "Someone sees you from above." [5]

Yes, without a doubt, we are being watched! Not by a cold and critical God who is watching and waiting for us to mess up so he can punish us. No, the God who is watching us is a good, loving, and merciful heavenly Father. Just knowing that this loving God has his eye on us is motivation to live our lives with wisdom and integrity.

It's a Heart Issue

Why is it that some people seem to have integrity, while others do not? The essence of integrity comes from what lies deep within our hearts and minds. As we said earlier, our actions often reveal what is in our hearts. Jesus himself said that outward actions are only the evidence of what lies beneath. "It is the thought-life that defiles you," he told his followers in Mark 7:20–22. "For from within, out of a person's heart, come evil thoughts, sexual immorality, theft, murder, adultery, greed, wickedness, deceit, eagerness for lustful pleasure, envy, slander, pride, and foolishness."

In Luke 6:43–45, Jesus makes a similar point: "A good tree can't produce bad fruit, and a bad tree can't produce good fruit. A tree is identified by the kind of fruit it produces. Figs never grow on thorn bushes or grapes on bramble bushes. A good person produces good deeds from a good heart, and an evil person produces evil deeds from an evil heart. Whatever is in your heart determines what you say."

According to Jesus, our words and actions must be sincere, and they must match up. We must not say, "I follow Christ" and then live in self-centeredness, anger, and dishonesty. If we say we're Christians, then we need to be the real deal. We need to live in obedience to Christ with sincerity and integrity. Here's how Jesus continues his discourse in Luke:

> So why do you call me "Lord," when you won't obey me? I will show you what it's like when someone comes to me, listens to my teaching, and then obeys me. It is like a person who builds a house on a strong foundation laid upon the underlying rock. When the floodwaters rise and break against the house, it stands firm because it is well built. But anyone who listens and doesn't obey is like a person who builds a house without a foundation. When the floods

sweep down against that house, it will crumble into a heap of ruins. (6:46–49)

We want to build our house on the rock, don't you? When we choose to walk in obedience to Christ and live lives full of integrity, we build our house—our lives—on a firm foundation that won't easily be shaken later in life.

Poor, Yet Rich

Maybe you're thinking, *I want to do what is right and live with integrity, but it's not that easy.* No kidding! It's hard for us too. So how can we as teenagers begin to develop hearts of integrity and lives that reflect obedience to Christ?

This is going to sound strange, but the secret to becoming rich in integrity is to become poor—poor in spirit, that is. In the Sermon on the Mount, Jesus taught his disciples how to be truly blessed. He began by saying, "Blessed are the poor in spirit, for theirs is the kingdom of heaven" (Matthew 5:3 NIV). The New Living Translation puts it this way: "God blesses those who realize their need for him, for the Kingdom of Heaven is given to them." To be good—truly good—we must first recognize our utter need for God. In and of ourselves, we are all fairly foolish and faulty creatures. Every single one of us has a deceptive heart. (If you don't think so, well, there's your evidence!) But God's Spirit at work in our lives can do powerful things.

Consider the Lord's words to Ezekiel. God commanded Ezekiel to tell his people, "I will give you a new heart with new and right desires, and I will put a new spirit in you. I will take out your stony heart of sin and give you a new, obedient heart. And I will put my Spirit in you so you will obey my laws and do whatever I command" (Ezekiel 36:26–27). What this passage tells us is that while our own hearts may be defective, God has a remedy: he wants to give us new hearts through our relationship with Jesus, by the power of his Holy Spirit. Will we accept those new hearts and be led by God's Spirit, or will we let our old hearts and fleshly desires dictate what we do and say?

In Romans 8:5–14, Paul wrote:

> Those who are dominated by the sinful nature think about sinful things, but those who are controlled by the Holy Spirit thing about things that please the Spirit. If your sinful nature controls your mind, there is death. But if the Holy Spirit controls your mind, there is life and peace. For the sinful nature is always hostile to God. It never did obey God's laws, and it never will. That's why those who are still under the control of their sinful nature can never please God.
>
> But you are not controlled by your sinful nature. You are controlled by the Spirit if you have the Spirit of God living in you. (And remember that those who do not have the Spirit of Christ living in them are not Christians at all.) Since Christ lives within you, even though your body will die because of sin, your spirit is alive because you have been made right with God. The Spirit of God, who raised Jesus from the dead, lives in you. And just as he raised Christ from the dead, he will give life to your mortal body by this same Spirit living within you.
>
> So, dear brothers and sisters, you have no obligation whatsoever to do what your sinful nature urges you to do. For if you keep on following it, you will perish. But if through the power of the Holy Spirit you turn from it and its evil deeds, you will live. For all who are led by the Spirit of God are children of God.

Here's the bottom line: if you are trying to live a life of integrity in your own power and strength, good luck! First of all, you're bound to run into pride problems if you think you can be good without God's help. And second, you're bound to fail. Only God can change our hearts, and only his Spirit at work within us enables us to live righteous lives. Apart from him we can do nothing. If we really want to be positive teens, the cry of our hearts has to be "Lord, I look to you. I want to be led by you. Cleanse my heart and help me to live the way I should through the power of your Spirit."

Clean Inside and Out

It's one thing to *look* good; it's another thing to *be* good. Teenagers can be pretty good at faking out their parents, teachers, and one another by keeping up an outward appearance of honesty and integrity. But we must be careful not to confuse showy outward actions with actions that come from an authentic, Christlike heart.

Back in Jesus's day, the Pharisees had a little trouble in this department. Oh, they followed all the rules and showed themselves to be as obedient as angels on the outside; but inside, their hearts were corrupted with deceit, bitterness, and jealousy. Here's the caution Jesus gave these religious leaders, who performed so perfectly when it came to following all the rules: "How terrible it will be for you teachers of religious law and you Pharisees. Hypocrites! You are so careful to clean the outside of the cup and the dish, but inside you are filthy—full of greed and self-indulgence! Blind Pharisees! First wash the inside of the cup, and then the outside will become clean, too" (Matthew 23:25–26).

To be positive teens, we need to keep a guard on our hearts and make sure we're not like the Pharisees, just living for show. Rather, we need to live for Christ and allow his light to shine authentically through our lives. A life of integrity is always lived from the inside out.

Integrity Shows!

About a year ago, our mother's alma mater, Baylor University, was in the news in a story that illustrated both integrity and the lack thereof. After the untimely and unfortunate death of one of Baylor's basketball players in the summer of 2003, allegations were made against Baylor involving both drugs and money in the athletic program. It was a dark day for the school, which was founded on biblical principles. The president of the university, Robert Sloan, pledged to begin an in-house investigation to look into the allegations. What started out as a not-so-pretty picture of dishonesty and compromise turned into a positive testimony of integrity for the Baylor president. On August 9, 2003, the article in the sports section of *The Dallas Morning News* read:

BAYLOR STEPS OUT OF FOG—PRESIDENT'S QUICK MOVE TO CLEAN HOUSE STOPS DEPARTMENT'S FREE FALL

In the midst of a summer darkened by tragedy, Baylor had a bright and shining moment on Friday. The school did the right thing by, as president Robert Sloan said, "putting its convictions into practice." Baylor set an example for every college athletic program by acting to restore integrity rather than just talking about it. The house cleaning started. . . . Baylor's administration did well in refusing to stonewall, alibi, stall, or duck responsibility. It acted with honor.[6]

What's the moral of the story? Integrity shows! It shows by our actions. It shows by our words. Even as teenagers, we can be bright, shining lights in the darkness of a sinful world by living with integrity at home, at school, and at work. Let's ask God right now to cleanse our hearts and fill us with his Holy Spirit. Then we can begin living positive lives of honesty and integrity—from the inside out.

POWER POINT

⚙ **Read:** Colossians 3:1–17. According to this passage, what actions should we put to death or get rid of in our lives? What qualities should we clothe ourselves with?

◉ **Pray:** Father, I praise you for your perfect integrity. You are without fault, and your Word can be trusted. Thank you for your Holy Spirit, who gives me the strength, day by day, to live a godly life. Make me new, Lord, from the inside out. Keep my feet on a straight path, and don't let me wander away from your principles. Lead me away from temptation and deliver me from evil. Help me to be a person of integrity—not so I can impress other people, but so others may be drawn to you by my good works. Glorify yourself in my life today and always. In Jesus's name I pray, amen.

💡 **Remember:** Colossians 3:17: "And whatever you do or say, let it be as a representative of the Lord Jesus, all the while giving thanks through him to God the Father."

☺ **Do:** Take a few quiet moments alone and write down areas in which you struggle with being honest. In what areas are you tempted to lie when the opportunity arises? Commit these areas to the Lord and ask him for the strength and courage to live with integrity.

8

Reinventing Honesty
Bringing Back the Basics of Truth

Unless we love the truth, we cannot know it.

—Blaise Pascal

I promise to tell the truth, the whole truth, and nothing but the truth—unless, of course, it will get me into trouble, inconvenience me, or embarrass me."

Unfortunately, that statement reflects the approach many people take to truth these days. During the past few decades, the foundational value of truth has been replaced in many lives by convenience and self-interest. Instead of asking, "What's the truth in this situation?" people ask, "What can I say that will get me off the hook?" In court, defendants place their hands on the Bible and swear to tell the truth, but then they don't follow through. And criminals aren't the only ones who are guilty of lying. Lately, the news has been full of stories about people in high offices, from politicians to chairmen of corporations to university athletic directors, who've proven they can't be trusted. It's hard to find someone who is willing to take a stand for truth anymore!

It's Always the Other Guy

Recently Michelle Malkin, columnist with Creators Syndicate, wrote a telling editorial that reveals how evasive truth can be, especially when we're busy pointing fingers at other people. Here's an excerpt from her column:

> Left-wing "comedian" Al Franken got tripped up by some big fat lies last week. He is sorry he got caught, but he is smugly silent about making fun of countless kids who have taken abstinence vows.
>
> Thanks to Court TV's Smoking Gun web site, we now know that the *Saturday Night Live* leftover abused his position as an "academic fellow" (now that's funny) at the Harvard University Kennedy School of Government's Shorenstein Center on the Press, Politics, and Public Policy in a puerile attempt to trick Attorney General John Ashcroft into publicly sharing his personal experience with abstinence.
>
> Mr. Franken urged Mr. Ashcroft to share his abstinence story for "a book about abstinence programs in our public schools entitled, *Savin' It!*" (lie). He assured Mr. Ashcroft that the book would document how the Bush administration is "setting the right example for America's youth" (lie). And he breezily informed Mr. Ashcroft that he already had "received wonderful testimonies from Health and Human Services Secretary Tommy Thompson, William J. Bennett, White House press secretary Ari Fleischer, Sen. Rick Santorum, and National Security Adviser Condoleezza Rice" (lie, lie, lie, lie, lie).
>
> Mr. Franken sent the bogus solicitation to Mr. Ashcroft on Harvard's letterhead earlier this summer, without the Shorenstein Center's knowledge or approval. A few weeks later, Mr. Franken sent an apology to Mr. Ashcroft. Mr.

Franken confessed that he had deliberately deceived Mr. Ashcroft while trying to gather material for his "satirical" anti-conservative book being rushed to print this month, *Lies and the Lying Liars Who Tell Them: A Fair and Balanced Look at the Right*. Mr. Franken sheepishly informed Mr. Ashcroft that the book will contain "only one or two chapters dealing with abstinence-only education."

"My biggest regret is sending the letter on Shorenstein Center stationery," Mr. Franken sniveled. "I am very embarrassed to have put them in this awkward and difficult position, and I ask you not to hold it against the center, the Kennedy School, or Harvard in general."

So, Mr. Franken is remorseful about offending his high-minded liberal benefactors at Harvard, who supported his book "research" under the guise of "bridging the gap between journalists and scholars" and "helping the press improve its role in democracy." But he has nothing to say about thoughtlessly ridiculing a growing movement that promotes self-restraint, strong morals, fidelity and good health.[1]

It doesn't seem to greatly bother Mr. Franken that he used deception and lies to add an interesting story to his book that, by its very title, is meant to point to the lies of others. But he does seem to be sorry that he used Harvard's letterhead to do it!

Oh, how easy it is to deceive ourselves into thinking that other people are the liars and that we're the truthful ones. We wish! The truth is, if we're going to expect honesty from others, then we must begin by being brutally honest with ourselves. Most teenagers would say that they value authenticity and truth. We expect to be told the truth, especially by adults; and we get offended or cynical when we discover that someone has been dishonest. Yet quite often, when we find ourselves in a tight situation, our love for truth somehow flutters away; and like everyone else, we say what's expedient, not what's truthful.

A recent report from the Josephson Institute of Ethics illustrates how far our generation has moved from the truth. Of the high-school students polled, 93 percent said that they had lied to a parent in the previous year; 83 percent reported that they had lied to a teacher. Seventy-four percent admitted to having cheated on a test.[2]

Maybe we need to take the log out of our own eye before grabbing for the speck in someone else's eye (see Matthew 7:4–5). That means being honest with ourselves as well as with others. After all, a positive teen is ultimately an honest teen. The question is, what can we do to keep dishonesty in check and build a firmer foundation of truth in our lives?

Why Truth?

As Christians we only have to look to Scripture to discover the foundational principles for positive living. Our Creator clearly set forth these basic principles in his Word. In the Old Testament, for example, God gave Moses a set of ten commandments designed to help the Israelites live with honor toward God and in harmony with one another. Number nine was this: "Do not testify falsely against your brother" (Exodus 20:16). Obviously, honesty is highly valued in God's book.

In fact, if we want to get a handle on just how much God despises deceit, we can turn to the book of Proverbs. Solomon had more than a few things to share with us on the subject of honesty:

- Proverbs 6:12–19: "Here is a description of worthless and wicked people: They are constant liars, signaling their true

Sin has many tools, but a lie is the handle that fits all of them. —Oliver Wendell Holmes

intentions to their friends by making signs with their eyes and feet and fingers. Their perverted hearts plot evil. They stir up trouble constantly. But they will be destroyed suddenly, broken beyond all hope of healing. There are six things the LORD hates—no seven things he detests: haughty eyes, a lying tongue, hands that kill the innocent, a heart that plots evil, feet that race to do wrong, a false witness who pours out lies, a person who sows discord among brothers."

- Proverbs 11:1: "The LORD hates cheating, but he delights in honesty."
- Proverbs 12:22: "The LORD hates those who don't keep their word, but he delights in those who do."
- Proverbs 19:5: "A false witness will not go unpunished, nor will a liar escape."
- Proverbs 19:9: "A false witness will not go unpunished, and a liar will be destroyed." (Apparently Solomon thought it was important to repeat this warning, in case we didn't catch it the first time!)
- Proverbs 20:10: "The LORD despises double standards of every kind."
- Proverbs 20:23: "The LORD despises double standards; he is not pleased by dishonest scales." (There he goes, repeating himself again!)

We'll finish on a more positive note:

- Proverbs 23:23: "Get the truth and don't ever sell it; also get wisdom, discipline and discernment."

Certainly these verses from Scripture give us plenty of motivation to stay honest! As Solomon said, liars will surely be caught in their lies. But the fear of getting caught can't be our only motivating factor. What's worse is what happens after we're caught. Other people find it difficult to trust us again. Our friends wonder if they can depend on our word. Our parents decide we're not trustworthy and curtail many of our freedoms. If our dishonesty continues and goes unchecked, then disregarding truth becomes easier and easier for us; and before we know it, we are exactly what we abhor in others: total frauds.

We need to value truth now! It's important for us to curb the urge to be deceitful while we're young, because dishonesty will only lead to trouble throughout our lives. Honesty, on the other hand, will lead to God's blessing. If we can learn now, as teenagers, to love truth and to stand on it, we can build a reputation of trust and respect that will serve us well in many areas as we grow older. For example, most of us want to have successful careers one day. Well, employers are looking for more than just aptitude and attitude; they want employees who are trustworthy too. They're most likely to hire and promote those people they know they can trust with their business. Honesty really is the best way to get ahead.

The Pressure to Cheat

OK, so you forgot about the history quiz today. It won't hurt just this once to ask your friend (who has the same teacher at an earlier period) to tell you what questions are on the quiz, right? Besides, you really need to score well to keep up your grade in that class. You spot your friend in the hallway and run to ask her about the quiz. But just as you're jotting down a few key points, you look up to see your history teacher walking in your direction, and she's not smiling. There goes your grade—along with a few other things, such as your honor and reputation.

Proverbs 11:1 says, "The LORD hates cheating, but he delights in honesty." Often we don't think of cheating as dishonesty. In our minds we rationalize, *Everyone is doing it*, or, *If I don't get a good grade on this test, my parents will kill me.* But cheating is lying, plain and simple. It's lying to the teacher. It's saying that we know certain information when in fact we do not.

Some people say, "What's the harm? I'm not hurting anyone." But that's not true. If you cheat, you hurt *you*. Not just because you haven't learned the stuff you need to know; that's a given. And not just because you may be humiliated and punished if you get caught.

The fact is, when you cheat and *don't* get caught, you start thinking that you can get away with dishonesty. If you can get away with cheating on a history test, then why not see if you can get away with cheating on a few responsibilities at home or at work? Then, when senior year rolls around, why not cheat on your college application? Most likely no one will ever know that you cheated your way into college—or through college. And then, what about your tax returns? Your business dealings? What's the big deal if you cheat a little bit to pad the bottom line? But it *is* a big deal. You've allowed yourself to be sucked into a lifestyle of dishonesty and deceit—and it all goes back to that history test.

In a lot of schools, the peer pressure to cheat can be huge. Not only is it tempting for us to cheat for our own gain, but it's also tempting to give a friend help through cheating. It takes courage and strength to take a stand and say, "That's wrong, and I'm not going to be a part of it."

Of course, Satan always seems to show up with a little voice that says, *It's not really that bad. Go ahead and do it.* That's when we need to remember what Peter told the early Christians: "Be careful! Watch out for attacks from the devil, your great enemy. He prowls around like a roaring lion, looking for some victim to devour. Take a firm stand against him, and be strong in your faith" (1 Peter 5:8–9). Are we willing to take a firm stand against cheating? Do we love honesty enough to guard against the temptation to cheat?

It doesn't matter if everyone else is doing it. As Christians, our lives ought to look a little different. Listen to Paul's encouragement in Ephesians 5:8–13:

> For though your hearts were once full of darkness, now you are full of light from the Lord, and your behavior should show it! For this light within you produces only what is good and right and true. Try to find out what is pleasing to the Lord. Take no part in the worthless deeds of evil and darkness; instead, rebuke and expose them. It is shameful even to talk about the things that ungodly people do in secret. But when the light shines on them, it becomes clear how evil these things are.

Why waste time and energy and risk our reputations to do something that's only going to ruin us in the long run? That's definitely not the way to become a positive teen!

Dishonesty—or Omission?

One Friday after school, Sarah asked her mom if she could spend the night at Amy's house. "Sure," her mom said. She had always liked Amy. What Sarah's mom didn't know, however, was that the two girls planned to go over to Beth's house later that night for a party. Beth had a reputation for wild parties, a fact that Sarah—and Sarah's mom—knew quite well.

Sarah's parents had a rule: Sarah had to tell them about any party she was invited to. She would be allowed to go only after they checked to make sure there would be parental supervision. *Hey, what Mom doesn't know won't hurt her. I'm not lying to her; I'm just not mentioning the party*, Sarah convinced herself.

Was Sarah being dishonest, or was she simply omitting the truth? Or are they both the same thing? It's tempting to play the "they didn't ask me" game and not reveal any truths that aren't specifically asked for. The question really comes down to this: did Sarah deceive her parents? Yes, she did. She was purposely trying to cover her actions. Her words weren't deceptive, because there were no words. Her actions were deceptive because she told a half-truth—she *was* sleeping at Amy's house that night, but she didn't tell her mom that she and Amy were going to Beth's party. As Proverbs 10:6 reminds us, "The godly are showered with blessings; evil people cover up their harmful intentions."

In Romans 13:12–13, Paul gives some healthy instructions to Christians: "The night is almost gone; the day of salvation will soon be here. So don't live in darkness. Get rid of your evil deeds. Shed them like dirty clothes. Clothe yourselves with the armor of right living, as those who live in the light. We should be decent and true in everything we do, so that everyone can approve of our behavior." Interestingly, this passage goes on to say something that would have been good for Sarah to hear. It could have motivated her to rethink her plans for Beth's party: "Don't participate in wild parties and getting drunk, or in adultery and immoral living, or in fighting and jealousy. But let the Lord Jesus Christ take control of you. And don't think of ways to indulge your evil desires" (Romans 13:13–14).

You see, honesty has to do with much more than words. If we're going to be 100 percent honest, truth must shine forth from our actions and deeds as well as our mouths. Perhaps you're thinking, *Oh, come on. You mean we can't keep anything from our parents?* No, that's not what we mean. We're saying that it's important to live in light and truth. If we're sneaking around doing something that we know our parents wouldn't approve of, that's deception. If you don't want to tell your mom that you have a crush on the new boy in English class, that's simply guarding your privacy. There's a big difference.

Truth stands the test of time; lies are soon exposed. —Proverbs 12:19

About Others

Possibly one of the most destructive temptations many teenagers face in the area of honesty is telling lies about other people. Mean girls, jealous boyfriends, social climbers, and disgruntled acquaintances can all get into this potentially devastating act of deception. Unfortunately, we can't prevent people from lying about us. We just have to trust our reputation to the Lord and ask him to keep it safely in his hands. But we *can* prevent ourselves from taking part in spreading lies about others. Not only are such lies terribly cruel to the victim; but eventually, when the truth comes out, the reputations of those who helped to disseminate the dishonesty are damaged.

Wise old Solomon (we go back to him a lot, don't we?) had a few things to say about people who lie about others:

- Proverbs 26:28: "A lying tongue hates its victims, and flattery causes ruin."
- Proverbs 25:18: "Telling lies about others is as harmful as hitting them with an ax, wounding them with a sword, or shooting them with a sharp arrow."

Wow! Do you want to be guilty of such violence? Not us!

Gossip fits into the category of spreading lies about others. Often, gossip is based on a little bit of truth mixed with a heaping portion of exaggeration or lies. And in God's arithmetic, a truth + an untruth = a lie. In Leviticus we read God's words to the Israelites: "Do not steal. Do not cheat one another. Do not lie. Do not use my name to swear a falsehood and so profane the name of your God. I am the LORD. Do not cheat or rob anyone. . . . Do not spread slanderous gossip among your people" (Leviticus 19:11–13, 16).

If we're going to be positive teens, we need to guard against using our words in a destructive way through gossip, slander, or falsehood. Instead of using our words to spread lies, we need to use them to do good and to bring healing to others. Proverbs 10:11 says, "The words of the godly lead to life." Paul's admonishment to the early Christians is a wonderful challenge to us:

> Don't use foul or abusive language. Let everything you say be good and helpful, so that your words will be an encouragement to those who hear them. And do not bring sorrow to God's Holy Spirit by the way you live. Remember, he is the one who has identified you as his own, guaranteeing that you will be saved on the day of redemption. Get rid of all bitterness, rage, anger, harsh words, and slander, as well as all types of malicious behavior. Instead, be kind to each other, tenderhearted, forgiving one another, just as God through Christ has forgiven you. (Ephesians 4:29–32)

Pure Honesty

Recently we were at a store that handed out free samples of dried mangoes. Oh, they tasted good! And the package read, "One Hundred Percent Naturally Sweet," which really made our sugar-conscious mom happy! So we bought two bags and munched away, thinking that we were eating a deliciously healthy snack, no sugar added.

When we got down to the final few mangoes in the first bag, we decided to check the ingredient label, expecting it to say "mangoes" and nothing else. Much to our surprise, however, the label listed a second main ingredient along with mangoes: sugar. *"One Hundred Percent Naturally Sweet"?* That package was only 50 percent honest!

Isn't that often the case when it comes to lying? More times than not, a lie contains a bit of truth. (Satan has been pulling this off since the Garden of Eden.) People redefine truth to allow for partial lies.

It's time for God-fearing young people to take a stand and reinvent honesty! Not partial honesty, but the full truth—so help us God. And that's the key: we need to ask God to help us keep our hearts and tongues pure. Perhaps our prayer can reflect the cry in Proverbs 30:7–8: "O God, I beg two favors from you before I die. First, help me never to tell a lie. Second, give me neither poverty nor riches. Give me just enough to satisfy my needs."

As we find our satisfaction in God, we have no need for lying. We can be honest with ourselves and with everyone else, because we know that God loves us and is watching over us. So with God's help, let's take a stand for truth that's not 50 percent, not 75 percent, but 100 percent pure. Let's make a new commitment to honesty in both word and deed, and set ourselves on the right road toward becoming positive teens.

POWER POINT

⚙ **Read:** Acts 5:1–10. Why did Ananias and Sapphira die? Was it because they didn't give all their money, or because they lied? Read verses 3–6 again. Who were they lying to?

◉ **Pray:** I praise you, wonderful God of truth! I know I can depend on your words, because they are true. Great is your faithfulness! Thank you for your Son, Jesus, who is the way, the truth, and the life. Help me to live, breathe, and speak the truth, and lead me away from the temptation to cheat, gossip, or deceive. Search me, God, and make my heart pure. Shine your light on the deceptions that need to be cleaned up in my life. Convict me and cleanse me. Make me honest! Thank you, Father, for I know that my help comes from you. In Jesus's name I pray, amen.

💡 **Remember:** Romans 13:13: "We should be decent and true in everything we do."

☺ **Do:** Make a decision right now about the value you will place on honesty in your life. On a note card, write out a statement of your personal commitment to uphold truth, and keep the card someplace where you will see it often. If you know you have said or done dishonest things, confess them to God, knowing that he forgives you through Christ (1 John 1:9). Don't wallow in regret, but move forward in God's strength to keep your commitment to honesty from this point on.

Power Principle #4

THe Power oF ReLAtioNshiP

A man wrapped up in himself makes a very small bundle.

—Benjamin Franklin

The most important commandment is this: "Hear, O Israel! The Lord our God is the one and only Lord. And you must love the Lord your God with all your heart, all your soul, all your mind, and all your strength." The second is equally important: "Love your neighbor as yourself." No other commandment is greater than these.

—Mark 12:29–31

Friends Forever
Developing Lasting Relationships in a Fast-Paced World

Two are better than one, because they have a good return for their work: If one falls down, his friend can help him up.

—Ecclesiastes 4:9–10 NIV

Have you ever been sitting in your car at the drive-thru window of a fast-food restaurant and thought to yourself, *What is taking so long?* It has been less than a minute, but somehow you are already tired of waiting! Our lightning-speed society demands everything quick. These days we have high-speed Internet connections, speed-dial telephones, and express checkouts, not to mention same-day dry cleaners, one-hour photo developing, ten-minute lube jobs, and two-minute microwavable cakes (don't try those!) And thank goodness for remote controls, because who has the patience to wait through a commercial break?

Without a doubt, our lives run at a hectic pace. But there is one thing that doesn't happen fast: friendship. Just like plants in a garden, friendships take time, effort, and care in order to grow. Good friendships don't happen overnight; they're a process. But because they are a vital, healthy, and positive part of our lives, friendships are worth everything we put into them.

Teenagers always want friends. In fact, some of us will go to great lengths to get them. The question is, to what end? Is our goal to have the most friends (quantity) or to have meaningful friendships (quality)? It's one thing to be popular and to be known by everyone; it's another thing to develop close, abiding, and loyal relationships. Sometimes, depending upon your personality and your priorities, you can do both.

Levels of Relationships

As we think about friendship, it helps to recognize that there are different levels of relationships in our lives. We can illustrate these levels with three concentric circles:

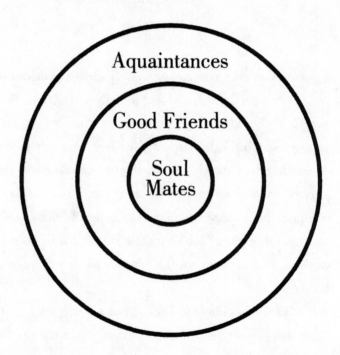

The outer circle represents the acquaintance level, which is made up of those people we know but not well. Generally speaking, conversations with acquaintances never get too deep. Everything stays on the surface: "Hi, how are you? How was Spanish class?"

We may have as many as two hundred acquaintances or as few as twenty-five, depending upon our personalities and activity levels. For instance, Ellie Extrovert has hundreds of acquaintances because she is a people person, loves to talk, and is involved in every club on campus. She never meets a stranger. Shy Shannon, on the other hand, has a much smaller number of acquaintances, because she doesn't feel comfortable talking with people she doesn't know. There's no good or bad here; being extroverted or shy or somewhere in-between is simply a function of how we're made. It's great to have lots of acquaintances, but it's also perfectly OK if we don't.

From this outer circle of acquaintances, we move in to the next, closer circle: good friends. Good friends are the ones we eat with at lunchtime, the ones we hang out with in the hallway before and after class, the ones we talk to on the phone; the ones we get together with on the weekend. With good friends, we have discovered a common bond. Something has connected, and the relationship has moved to a deeper level.

Most people have anywhere from five to twenty-five good friends throughout their lifetimes. Those may sound like small numbers. But the fact is, it's better to have a handful of good friends than dozens of superficial ones. As Proverbs 18:24 says, "A man of many companions may come to ruin." What Solomon was probably getting at is this: maintaining a large number of good friends is difficult, since deeper relationships require more time and attention than acquaintance-level relationships. We can't please everyone. When we try to have too many close companions or good friends, we end up running around frantically trying to maintain each relationship. Eventually we fall apart. There's only so much of us to go around! Another wise man, Aristotle, put it well: "A friend to all is a friend to none."[1]

Jesus understood this principle. He had numerous acquaintances, but he also had a smaller, closer circle of friends: his disciples, Nicodemus, Mary, Martha, Lazarus, and John the Baptist. These were

Friends are the sunshine of life. —John Hay

the people he chose to spend time with and grow closer to in friendship. He knew better than to try to be all things to all people.

The innermost of the three concentric circles represents the deepest level of relationship possible. We call the people in this circle "soul mates." Some people call them "best friends." These are the heart-to-heart friends with whom we can share anything. We cry, laugh, get angry, and rejoice with these special friends. Even when soul mates move away and we don't talk to them for months or even years, in the next conversation, we seem to pick up right where we left off.

Because we spend more time nurturing and growing these special relationships, they are deeper and richer than other relationships and often last a lifetime. (One day when you get married, your spouse will fit into this category.) If we have two or three soul mates in our lives, we can count ourselves blessed!

Jesus had this inner circle of soul mates with Peter, James, and John. He always took these three friends with him to share his most significant events. They were the ones he invited to go to the mountaintop to witness the Transfiguration. They were also the ones he asked to stay close when he prayed in the Garden of Gethsemane, just before going to the cross.

From Lonely to Meaningful

So how do these relationships develop? How do people go from being acquaintances to good friends to possibly soul mates? Do these things just *happen*? Well, sometimes they do. Sometimes God puts people together, and an instant connection seems to take place. But generally speaking, relationship building takes effort from both parties.

This is important to remember, because friends move in and out of our lives for various reasons. Loneliness hits all of us now and then. When it does, the best, most positive antidote is to make an effort to reach out to someone else—to take that first step to cross the bridge from acquaintance to good friend or from good friend to best friend. How? Well, as our grandmothers used to say, "Honey, in order to have friends, you must show yourself friendly." In other words, in order to be positive teens who are capable of developing deeper friendships, we must demonstrate the qualities of a good friend.

What qualities are we talking about? Here are the top five. As you read these, do a little self-examination. Ask God to build these qualities into your life as you reach out to the people around you.

Be Others-Oriented

Sometimes we get comfortable staying in our own little box, and then we wonder why we're so lonely! We may just need to pry our eyes off of ourselves and start getting interested in other people. What do they love? What are they interested in? What do they enjoy doing? As we get our focus off of what *we* want and how *we* feel, and think instead about how we can make another person's life better, we can begin to extend the wonderful hand of true friendship.

Dale Carnegie, author of *How to Win Friends and Influence People*, said, "You can make more friends in two months by becoming interested in other people than you can in two years by trying to get people interested in you." [2] The apostle Paul had the same idea when he wrote, "Don't be selfish; don't live to make a good impression on others. Be humble, thinking of others as better than yourself. Don't think only about your own affairs, but be interested in others, too, and what they are doing. Your attitude should be the same that Christ Jesus had" (Philippians 2:3–5).

Be Joyful

Sometimes we just need to lighten up! Enjoy life. Enjoy your friends. Smile. Laugh together. Do fun things together. Most people need someone they can not only cry with, but someone they can laugh with too—someone with whom they can share fun times. The Bible tells us over and over again to rejoice! But we get so caught up in *stuff*. Whether it's a bad grade, hurt feelings, or a well-deserved punishment, the stuff of life can get us down and keep us from being the kind of person others would want to be around. That's why we need to make a conscious choice to get out of the pits and focus on what we can be grateful for!

Can't think of a reason to be grateful? Here's one that's always available to us as Christians: even when we think we have no friends, we always have the perfect friend in Jesus. We can turn all our burdens, worries, and cares over to him. Instead of allowing our negative feelings to rule us, we can release those feelings to Christ, ask him to fill us with his joy, and then go out and do something that brings joy to someone else. It's a simple fact that whenever we pour ourselves into bringing joy to others, we can't keep that joy from coming back on us!

For example, one of the things that gives us a lot of joy personally is our volunteer work with Special Olympics, the international program that provides athletic training and competition for disabled kids and adults around the world. If you ever need something to lift your spirits, just spend a day with a group of Special Olympians! Every time we devote an afternoon to hugging and cheering on these precious athletes, their effortless, infectious joy becomes our own.

Be Loyal

Proverbs 17:17 (NIV) tells us, "A friend loves at all times." Based on that definition, we wonder: how many of us are true friends? Unfortunately, loyalty—loving at all times—is a rare commodity in today's world. Many people, teenagers included, don't have the courage to stand by a friend, especially if that friend is being ridiculed or abandoned by "the crowd." But a friend who is not loyal is really no friend at all. Loyalty is the most important gift one friend can give to another.

How do we show loyalty? For one thing, by guarding our mouths. Gossip is so tempting; but when we participate in gossip about a friend, we destroy that friendship with just a few loose words. Just because a story is true doesn't mean that it needs to be shared! Besides, if someone is gossiping to us about a friend, that person is most likely talking about us behind our backs too. That's not the kind of friend we want to have—or the kind of friend we want to be.

It has been said, "He who proves himself true to one friend, thus proves himself worthy of many."[3] Being the one who speaks up and says, "Hey, don't make fun of Mary. I like her," or, "Don't say that about Rob. He's a good guy," isn't easy. But when we take a stand—even when it seems like the unpopular thing to do—we prove that we are loyal friends. And there's a bonus: people eventually leave gossipers and ridiculers and flock to those people who've proven to be loyal and trustworthy.

Granted, sometimes friendships fade. People and circumstances change. Loyalty doesn't mean keeping all the same friends forever. However, it *does* mean choosing not to talk about our friends, past or present, behind their backs. It means refusing to betray their trust in any way—no matter what.

Jesus knew the pain of having a good friend betray him (Judas) and a close friend deny their friendship (Peter). When those things happen to us, we need to reject the urge to get back at the person who hurt us. Instead, we need to take our pain and anger to Jesus. He cries with us and understands our hurts. He alone can help us forgive and move on.

Overlook Faults

Thomas Fuller once said, "We shall never have friends if we expect to find them without fault."[4] His comment echoes an old Turkish proverb: "He who seeks a perfect friend, remains without one." The fact is, everyone has his or her own little annoyances and idiosyncrasies. We have them, and our friends have them. We must be willing to overlook our friends' weaknesses and shortcomings, just as we hope they are willing to overlook ours. If we choose to get annoyed by every little thing that others do, we will soon find that we have very few friends indeed!

God's example of grace toward us should give us the inspiration we need to look past the faults of others. Because of Christ's death on the cross, God looks past our sins and sees us in the wonderful state of forgiveness. Friendship grows when we look upon other people with that same grace.

Overlooking faults, however, does not mean staying indefinitely in an unhealthy relationship. If we find that a friend is consistently disloyal to us, then we need to distance ourselves from that person. Other matters of dishonesty or rebellion against authority may also trigger a reason for concern. We'll touch on this idea in the next section. When we say it is important to overlook faults, we are not talking about overlooking sin. Sin needs to be dealt with and should not be ignored.

What if you find yourself having a problem with a particular friend? Let's say a girl you've known for some time has done you wrong. It's a good idea to confront her quietly. Confronting your friend allows you to be completely honest with her and may, in fact, save the friendship. Avoiding the problem, on the other hand, may break up the relationship. Handle confrontation carefully and prayerfully. Not everything needs to be an issue, so use discernment on what is important enough to confront. If you make it a practice to constantly confront friends about small stuff, you won't have many friends for long.

Be Genuine

Sometimes we think we need to put on a mask and pretend we're something that we're not in order for people to like us. Not so! Friends gravitate to those who are the real deal, not phonies or pretenders. No one wants a friend who's a fake. We all want friends who are open, honest, and consistent in what they say, believe, and do. It's a real turn-off to friendship when a person is one way with one set of people and another way with another set.

Of course, being genuine doesn't give us an excuse to be irresponsible and negative and then say, "That's just the way I am." Be yourself, but be your best self! If you feel like whining all the time, don't do it under the guise of being genuine. Instead, stop whining and choose to be grateful and joyful. Ultimately, the key to being genuine is not to live by the whims of our feelings, but by the consistency of our positive choices.

Choose Your Companions Wisely

To be brutally honest, not everyone makes a good friend. There are some people who may actually be a detrimental influence in our lives. Scripture warns us about choosing good companions. Solomon said, "Whoever walks with the wise will become wise; whoever walks with fools will suffer harm" (Proverbs 13:20).

When it comes to the people we hang out with, we need to choose wisely, since the Bible says we will become just like the ones we walk with in life. Paul warned the early Christians of this very danger when he said, "Don't be fooled . . . 'bad company corrupts good character'" (1 Corinthians 15:33). Unfortunately, it's human nature for the bad to bring down the good. Sometimes the good can bring up the bad, but those instances are rare. Don't be fooled!

As iron sharpens iron, a friend sharpens a friend. —Proverbs 27:17

That's not to say we should be *judgmental* toward other people. Rather, we should be *discerning*. If certain friends have chosen to pursue foolish or dangerous lifestyles, then we must stop hanging out with them. That doesn't mean we should be rude and turn against them. But in as kind a manner as possible, we must simply stop going places and doing things with them.

Some time ago a friend of ours became involved in the wrong crowd. Kory (not her real name) began doing drugs and moving far away from her Christian roots due to the influence of her new friends. Yet God did an amazing transformation in her life, and Kory eventually had a complete turnaround in her heart. She started hanging out with a whole new crowd—a group of strong Christians who helped her stay on the right path. She has been living for the Lord ever since and has been a positive and powerful influence on others, including her old friends.

To become positive teens, we need to be cautious about our companions. In our circle of acquaintances, there is room for all types of people. But we must choose wisely when it comes to those we draw into our circle of good friends—those we spend the bulk of our time with. As James Howell said long ago, "Choose thy friends like thy books, few but choice."[5]

The Perfect Friend

Have you ever let someone down? Maybe they needed to talk, and you were too busy. Or maybe you weren't loyal with your words or deeds. We all have regrets in friendships, because we all make mistakes.

Perhaps you can think of a time in your life when a friend let *you* down. The fact is, there are no perfect friends. None of our friends can be there for us 24/7. None can always listen to us and offer all the wisdom we need. None are perfectly faithful, perfectly loving, or perfectly forgiving—except one.

As we said earlier, Jesus is the only perfect friend. He's the only one who fits the bill. He is always there for us. His love is perfect, abundant, joyful, genuine, and loyal. Scripture is filled with God's words of love for us. Here are two of our favorites:

- Romans 8:35–40: "Can anything ever separate us from Christ's love? Does it mean he no longer loves us if we have trouble or calamity, or are persecuted, or are hungry or cold or in danger or threatened with death? (Even the Scriptures say, 'For your sake we are killed every day; we are being slaughtered like sheep.') No, despite all these things, overwhelming victory is ours through Christ, who loved us. And I am convinced that nothing can ever separate us from his love. Death can't, and life can't. The angels can't, and the demons can't. Our fears for today, our worries about tomorrow, and even the powers of hell can't keep God's love away. Whether we are high above the sky or in the deepest ocean, nothing in all creation will ever be able to separate us from the love of God that is revealed in Christ Jesus our Lord."

- 1 John 3:1–2: "See how very much our heavenly Father loves us, for he allows us to be called his children, and we really are! But the people who belong to this world don't know God, so they don't understand that we are his children. Yes, dear friends, we are already God's children, and we can't even imagine what we will be like when Christ returns. But we do know that when he comes we will be like him, for we will see him as he really is."

It's only by really understanding how much God loves us that we become positive friends and positive teens. By grasping the full depth and breadth of God's love for us, we become much more confident and much less needy in all our relationships. What's more, we begin to allow God's grace-filled love to overflow from our hearts to those around us. And that amazing love, demonstrated to us and through us, is a wonderful, powerful, and positive thing.

POWER POINT

⚙ **Read:** John 15:1–17. Describe the kind of relationship Jesus wants to have with each of us. How do you think you can develop that kind of relationship? What does Jesus command us to do in this passage?

◉ **Pray:** Glorious, loving heavenly Father, I praise you for your faithful love toward me. I am grateful that you are always with me and that you always care. Thank you for the friends you have brought into my life. Love them through me. Help me to be a better friend by reaching out and taking a genuine interest in others. Please give me the ability and strength to be loyal, genuine, forgiving, and positive. I praise you and thank you for being the perfect friend. I rejoice in your love. In Jesus's name I pray, amen.

💡 **Remember:** John 15:12: "I command you to love each other in the same way that I love you."

😊 **Do:** Take another look at the concentric-circles diagram in this chapter, then create your own relationship diagram on a blank sheet of paper. In the outer circle, write the names of some of the acquaintances in your life. (Don't spend too much time with this; just write down the names that come to mind quickly.) In the middle circle, write the names of your good friends. Finally, in the inner circle, list those people who are your true soul mates. As you look at these circles, pray and ask God to show you those acquaintances and friends you can grow closer to. Examine the qualities of a good friend described in this chapter, and make a commitment to develop and strengthen these qualities in your own life.

10

Family Feud
Harmony on the Home Front

Live in harmony with each other. Don't try to act important, but enjoy the company of ordinary people. And don't think you know it all!

—Romans 12:16

So your family's not perfect. Join the club! Even though some families may *look* perfect from the outside, we can tell you right now: they're not. Every family has its challenges, problems, and struggles to one degree or another. That's because every family is made up of faulty, sinful people who have both strengths and flaws. No family is immune to conflict.

You may be thinking, *But you don't know my family. We don't get along at all. If there were a magazine about dysfunctional families, we'd be the cover story.* You're right. We don't know your exact situation. But we do know that God sees everything, and he knows what you are going through. He is with you, and he wants to help you. You are not alone.

Or maybe you're thinking, *I have a pretty nice, normal family. I can't complain; a lot of kids are in worse boats. So why do I get so annoyed with my parents? And shouldn't I be able to get along better with my sister?* You're not alone either. Even in the best of families, family relationships can be confusing during the teenage years. The question is, how do we stay positive through family issues and struggles that can sometimes seem stranger than fiction?

Understanding Them

Do you ever wish that your parents would simply understand you—just once? We know we have! But have you ever turned the tables and thought about trying to understand your parents? A line in a famous prayer attributed to Saint Francis of Assisi goes like this: "Grant that I may not so much seek . . . to be understood as to understand." Actually, your parents may understand you better than you think; after all, they were once teenagers too.

It's scary to think that our parents just might have a little more insight into us than we have into them. Of course, they've had the benefit of the thousands of books that have flooded the market during the last couple of decades telling them how to love, communicate, and raise their teenagers. We can't help but wonder, *What's so wrong with us that they need all those books anyway?* To be honest, when Mom brought home the book *Parenting Teenagers for Dummies,* we both thought we would lose it! Are we really that difficult? OK, OK; maybe we *are* a little temperamental at times and argue and whine on occasion; but is that book really necessary? Maybe someone should write a book for teenagers called *Dealing with Overly Concerned Parents for Dummies!*

As we've considered this idea of parent/teenager understanding, we've identified what we think are the two major issues that teenagers really need to understand about their parents. If we get these two, a lot of other things about Mom and Dad will make more sense:

1. Generally speaking, parents teach us, train us, and discipline us because they love us and want us to grow up to be successful adults one day. The rules that parents lay down may seem annoying, frustrating, and downright unfair, but usually Mom and Dad aren't setting boundaries just to be cruel to us. In fact, the easiest thing for them would be to let us go and do as we please. But because they love us (and yes, because they do have a little understanding of us), they make rules and set limits.

Scripture reminds us that God deals with his own children the same way. Proverbs 3:11–12 says, "My child, don't ignore it when the LORD disciplines you, and don't be discouraged when he corrects you. For the LORD corrects those he loves, just as a father corrects a child in whom he delights." God lovingly works with us, teaching us, training us, and disciplining us for our own good. We are not to despise that discipline, which is a manifestation of his great love for us. With our heavenly Father, love and discipline go hand in hand. The same is true with our earthly mothers and fathers.

2. Parents are imperfect people like the rest of us, but they are also our God-given authorities. Our parents are human too. They're not perfect— and most of them don't claim to be. They have faults and weaknesses, and most likely they will make some mistakes in parenting. (So will we when it's our turn.) We need to relate to them with a healthy dose of mercy, forgiveness, and understanding.

At the same time, we need to accept the fact that our parents are the ones God has placed in authority in our families. Ephesians 6:1–3 says, "Children, obey your parents because you belong to the Lord, for this is the right thing to do. 'Honor your father and mother.' This is the first of the Ten Commandments that ends with a promise. And this is the promise: If you honor your father and mother, 'you will live a long life, full of blessing.'"

All of our lives we will face authority figures who are far from perfect, from teachers to bosses to politicians. Nevertheless, we must honor the authorities God has placed over us. And that begins with our parents.

There is no perfect parent except God himself. And the fact is, our perfect heavenly Father set our earthly parents in authority over us, knowing that they have both strengths and weaknesses. When we honor our parents, we honor God. We also become recipients of God's blessing.

Understanding Ourselves

If we really want our parents to understand us, we need to make sure we understand ourselves first! Again, we've identified two big issues that we need to acknowledge about ourselves as teenagers. We're talking in generalities, of course; but if we're honest, most of us would admit (painfully, perhaps) that we have these two points in common:

1. No matter how smart we think we are, we really don't know it all. In fact, let's go ahead and admit it: our parents have lived a little more of life than we have. And although they may not know the names of our favorite rock groups or movie stars, they have probably learned one or two things from their life experiences that we don't know yet. Proverbs 15:5 says, "Only a fool despises a parent's discipline; whoever learns from correction is wise."

2. We're in a transition time in our lives. We're almost adults, but then again, we're still kids. We want to be independent in most ways, but we find ourselves still dependent in other ways. All teenagers go through stages of defiance in their attitudes and actions to one degree or another. What this demands is that we use self-control in our relationships with others—and especially with our families. As Ephesians 4:26 reminds us, "In your anger do not sin."

There now, we have honestly placed on the table a few stark realities about both parents and teens. That wasn't so hard, was it? Now the question is, how do we use this insight to get along a little bit better with our family members?

Positive Conflicts

It's inevitable. Conflict is going to happen in every family, because every family is made up of faulty people. (Yes, that includes us.) Being

Rejoice with your family in the beautiful land of life. —Albert Einstein

122

so close in age, as sisters we have gone through times where it seems we are constantly fighting. However, instead of feeling like failures because we've had an argument with a parent or a sibling, we need to accept the fact that disagreements are going to occur in family settings. The important thing is how we handle these disagreements.

For example, arguing with family members (or anyone else, for that matter) should not be about winning or losing. It should be about making sure that the other person understands our viewpoint and that we understand his or her viewpoint as well. We may be able to come to an equitable resolution; then again, we may not. We may end up agreeing to disagree. But that's OK. Sometimes issues seem to sift themselves out over time.

As we work through conflicts in our families, here are some rules to remember:

Do

- use a respectful tone of voice.
- stick with the facts.
- guard your tongue from saying something that you will regret later.
- be willing to apologize when necessary or to accept an apology.
- ask God to give you wisdom and direction.
- use self-control and gentleness to get your point across.
- seek to understand the other person.
- make it your goal to be understood, not necessarily to win.
- be willing to forgive, forget, and move on.

Don't

- use cutting or hurtful words, especially those aimed at someone's character.
- be selfish.

- bring up past hurts.
- exaggerate or lie.
- yell or scream.
- beat a subject to death or repeat the same things over and over again.
- argue about everything; pick your battles carefully.

Not everything needs to be an issue for argument. Sometimes we need to love sacrificially, take a big gulp, and let an issue pass. Sometimes, even though we don't like what our parents have told us to do, we need to accept their authority without putting up a fight. Laying down our right to argue is not a sign of weakness but rather a sign of strength. It's an act of self-sacrifice and self-control. It's also an act that follows the example of Jesus, who laid down all of his rights when he allowed himself to be crucified on the cross.

In Matthew 5:39, Jesus tells us to turn the other cheek when someone offends us. And in Matthew 5:9 he says, "God blesses those who work for peace, for they will be called the children of God." Paul adds this exhortation in Romans 12:17–21:

> Never pay back evil for evil to anyone. Do things in such a way that everyone can see you are honorable. Do your part to live in peace with everyone, as much as possible.
>
> Dear friends, never avenge yourselves. Leave that to God. For it is written, "I will take vengeance; I will repay those who deserve it," says the Lord.
>
> Instead, do what the Scriptures say: "If your enemies are hungry, feed them. If they are thirsty, give them something to drink, and they will be ashamed of what they have done to you." Don't let evil get the best of you, but conquer evil by doing good.

As this passage makes clear, we don't have to fight about every issue, and we certainly shouldn't take it upon ourselves to get "payback."

Instead we ought to selflessly and humbly examine what is worth going to battle over—and what is not. Before we engage in conflict with our parents, siblings, or other family members, we need to ask ourselves, *Will it be worth it?* Stopping to reflect isn't easy; most of us would much rather blow up on the spot. But self-control is possible in God's strength. His power at work in our lives can give us love, patience, and restraint far beyond our own abilities.

Respectful Submission

What about those times when we think our parents are being cruel and unusual in their rules or punishment? After all, as we said earlier, parents aren't perfect. What if we think they've made a mistake?

When Scripture tells us to honor our parents, it doesn't mean that we have no voice in matters that affect us. It does mean that our voice must be kind, humble, and respectful. Most parents are approachable, if the approach is done in a respectful way. Here are six steps we recommend from our own experience (and after discussions with Mom about "what works"):

1. Determine if the issue is really worth bringing up. Before you argue that a particular rule or punishment is unfair, put yourself in your parents' shoes and try to understand why they may have put the rule or punishment in place. If you do this and still believe you've been misunderstood, unfairly treated, or wrongfully punished, then you might want to bring up the issue.

2. Arrange a time and place to talk. Tell your parents that you want to discuss something with them and that you need fifteen minutes of their undivided attention (or some other specific amount of time).

3. Begin your approach with understanding. It's important to start by telling your parents that you understand their viewpoint (as much as possible, anyway). For example, say, "Mom and Dad, I understand why you want my curfew to be 11:30 on a weekend night, since that seems to be a reasonable time for me to be safely home, but . . ."

4. Present your request clearly, concisely, and logically. "I would like to ask you to consider changing my curfew to midnight, because many school dances and movies finish at 11:30, and I need a little more time to get home."

5. Provide assurance. "I want to assure you that I am not going to do anything to disobey you; I'm simply asking that you consider my request. I promise I will be responsible and be home at or before whatever curfew you set."

6. Be appreciative. Thank your parents for being willing to listen to you and to work with you. And don't huff and grumble if things don't go your way right away. Give your parents time to consider what you have presented. You might even tell them, "I don't expect you to give me an answer right now. You can let me know later, after you've had time to discuss it."

When we follow these six steps, we show our parents that we are responsible, respectful, and self-controlled. (In the future, the same procedure will help resolve conflicts with college professors and bosses.) These steps also give us an opportunity to reflect on our parents' viewpoint. And here's a key: Whatever the outcome, we must always be open to what God wants to teach us in a situation. If our parents come back with "no" for an answer, we must accept it, knowing that God placed our parents in our lives on purpose, and we did what we could. We can save ourselves a lot of grief by keeping our eyes on the bigger picture—the eternal one—which promises God's blessing for those who honor God by honoring their parents. After all, in view of eternity, does the issue we're concerned about really matter?

They Annoy Me!

Sometimes our conflicts aren't really conflicts at all. They don't have to do with issues; they have to do with personalities—and personalities often clash. We brush off a parent or sibling or friend by saying, "He (or she) annoys me." Well, here's a news flash: everyone is annoying in some form or fashion. Every single person on the face of this earth has something about him or her that bugs someone else!

What bugs us about a particular person may be OK with you. On the other hand, we may be fine with someone's odd traits, while those same quirks completely annoy you. Still, most teenagers would probably agree: we are never so annoyed as by our siblings. What is it about brothers and sisters that drives us nuts? Could it be that we are around them so much that their little flaws seem large to us? Could it be that we are jealous of them, or just tired of their personalities? Whatever the reason for our annoyance, most of us could use a little dose of sibling *forbearance*.

What in the world is forbearance? Colossians 3:13 (NIV) tells us, "Bear with each other and forgive whatever grievances you may have against one another. Forgive as the Lord forgave you." The New Living Translation puts it this way: "You must make allowance for each other's faults and forgive the person who offends you. Remember, the Lord forgave you, so you must forgive others." Are we willing to make allowances for the faults of our brothers and sisters? Granted, it's not easy. But if God can look with grace toward us, then surely we ought to do the same for others—especially to those living under our same roof.

How do we forbear with our brothers and sisters? First, by asking

Politeness, that cementer of friendship and soother of enmities, is nowhere so much required, and so frequently outraged, as in family circles. —Marguerite Blessington

God to pour out his love for them through us. God's love covers a multitude of sins. The Bible tells us the key to love:

> All who proclaim that Jesus is the Son of God have God living in them and they live in God. We know how much God loves us, and we have put our trust in him.
>
> God is love and all who live in love live in God, and God lives in them. . . .
>
> If someone says, "I love God," but hates a Christian brother or sister, that person is a liar; for if we don't love people we can see, how can we love God, whom we have not seen? And God himself has commanded that we must love not only him but our Christian brothers and sisters too. (1 John 4:15–16, 20–21)

The second way we forbear is by focusing on our family members' good points and overlooking some of their negatives. We need to look for and dwell on the best in our brothers, sisters, and other family members, because we want them to do the same for us!

There's one important caveat we need to mention: if you are in an abusive situation with a family member, you must get help. When we say that we should forbear with one another, we don't mean that we should overlook a family member's aggressive or destructive sin. If you're in a situation where you are being physically, emotionally, or sexually abused by someone in your family, we encourage you to talk to a trusted and godly adult today. And take heart in the knowledge that God is your true Father. Parents will never meet all of our needs or fulfill all of our hopes. In Christ alone is our comfort and strength. God is the ultimate parent.

Traits of a Healthy Family

We want to close this chapter with a picture of what a healthy family looks like. (We're not saying "perfect family," because we all know there aren't any.) Healthy families typically have ten traits that distinguish them:

1. They have an exceptional commitment to each member of the family.

2. They communicate with truth and grace.

3. They affirm the value and uniqueness of each member of the family.

4. They vow never to abuse, shame, control, or intimidate one another.

5. They share a strong spiritual foundation.

6. They teach respect for others.

7. They instill a sense of responsibility in one another.

8. They play together.

9. They celebrate rituals and traditions together.

10. They seek help when they come to an impasse.[1]

As we seek to be positive teens, let's work on developing these ten traits within our current family structures. Maybe you're thinking, *But my family doesn't look anything like a healthy family.* Don't worry. We must take what we have been given and do the best we can with it, seeking God's guidance in the relationship-building process. Later we can practice the ten traits in our own families, when *we* are the parents. With God's help, these wonderful qualities can continue to pass on from generation to generation! After all, God places us in families on purpose. Treating family members with love, respect, and forbearance is the most positive thing we can do.

POWER POINT

Read: 1 Corinthians 13. According to this passage, why is love important? Underline the words that describe true love. Is this kind of love possible? Read 1 John 4:16. Where does love come from?

Pray: God of love, I praise you for your abundant and merciful love toward me! You are faithful, and your love is sure and true. Thank you that you live inside of me and your love can be reflected in my life. Pour out your grace-filled love through me to my family members. Help me to honor and respect my parents as I honor and respect you. Grant me the ability to forbear and make allowances for the faults of my siblings. Thank you that you satisfy all my needs. May I walk in your love moment by moment! In Jesus's name I pray, amen.

Remember: 1 John 4:7: "Dear friends, let us continue to love one another, for love comes from God. Anyone who loves is born of God and knows God."

Do: Read through 1 Corinthians 13 again and identify some "love areas" that you personally need to work on with your family members. Ask for God's help and determine to show a difference in your family relationships this week. If you have any issues that you need to bring up with your parents, use the steps in this chapter to make your respectful petition.

The Dating Game
Survival Tips and Tools for Success

The person you're dating is a unique creation of God.
He made only one of each of you, and as much as
He loves you, He loves the person you're with, too.
Treat that person like he/she is one of a kind.

—Susie Shellenberger and Greg Johnson

Reality dating show mania has hit the airwaves. Could the networks possibly think up one more spin on *The Bachelor* and *The Bachelorette*? *Joe Millionaire* was creative, we suppose. Then there was *For Love or Money, Perfect Match,* and *Outback Jack.* These shows may be "reality TV," but in reality no one wants dating to be the sort of cruel game we see on television.

Dating can be a wonderful experience—one that allows us to grow and mature in our understanding of and relationships with the opposite sex. Dating gives us opportunities to learn how to relate, communicate, and deal with the sometimes difficult issues that arise between girls and guys. Done right, dating can be purposeful, fun, and a blessing in our lives. Done wrong, it can be a drain and a distraction from God's purpose for us.

When should you open the door to dating? This is a decision you should make with your parents. You need to consider many factors, including your maturity and the character of your potential date. Your community or the people you are around make a difference too.

Dallas, where we live, is a very big city, but we mostly hang around a smaller community of families we know from church and school. It's an everyone-knows-everyone kind of situation, which creates accountability.

Generally speaking, the purpose of dating is to prepare us for a marriage relationship down the road—to help us sort out some of the qualities we like and don't like in a potential marriage partner. Since dating can lead to falling in love, which can lead to marriage, we need to guard our hearts and date wisely. Let's look at some keys to successful dating.

Living in Reality

Most likely you fall into one of two categories: you either want a boyfriend (or girlfriend), or you have one. Most teenagers feel a little tug in their hearts to be in a dating relationship. But why? Have you ever thought about why you want that kind of attachment in your life? Here are some possibilities:

1. You want a boyfriend or girlfriend because you think he or she will make you feel more secure as a person. Interestingly enough, there's not as much security in having a boyfriend or girlfriend as you may think. For one thing, there is no guarantee that the person you are going out with will want a long-term relationship. A breakup will come at some point, unless you are one of those rare, rare few who marry their high-school sweethearts. A dating relationship can (and most likely will) shift and change. It's not a stable place to put your hope for security.

The truth is, your security needs to come from within. It needs to come from an inner God-confidence—from a deep knowing that God loves you immensely and will never leave you. Of course, you may find

Lead a life worthy of your calling, for you have been called by God. —Ephesians 4:1

it difficult to say, "I don't want a boyfriend (or girlfriend), because all my needs are met in Christ." The world constantly tells us that we should be in a relationship and that something must be wrong with us if we're not. The second part of that statement isn't true, but God *does* intend for most of us to have a life partner. Our yearnings in that direction are natural and God-given.

The important thing to realize is that a boyfriend or girlfriend can never meet all your needs for love and security. He or she can't take the place of God in your life.

2. You want a boyfriend or girlfriend because you think it will make you popular. Trust us, if you have to have a boyfriend or girlfriend to be popular, you may want to rethink being popular. If the way to move up the ladder of popularity is to use people to get there, you may have chosen the wrong ladder to climb!

Consider why you want to be popular. Is it so everyone will like you? Well, here's a little inside scoop: even popular people aren't liked by everyone. Don't use a boyfriend or girlfriend as your ticket to fame and popularity. Be a kind, fun, and genuine person, and enjoy the loyal friends who come your way as a result.

3. You want a boyfriend or girlfriend because everyone else has one. OK, we don't live in your town. We don't go to your school. But we do know that it's highly unlikely (more like impossible) that every single teenager you know is going out with someone. Granted, it may seem as if everyone is dating except you; but take a closer look. The truth is, many teenagers are not part of a couple, and they would love to get together in groups to do fun things. Find those people, get together, have fun, and stop sulking and thinking that you're the only one without a boyfriend or girlfriend.

4. You want a boyfriend or girlfriend because you want someone with whom you can have a physical relationship. Wrong motive. Totally based on hormones, not wisdom. Don't even go there.

5. *You want a boyfriend or girlfriend because you think having one will make you happy.* Much like the security thing, you can't depend on someone else to give you happiness. You can't let your emotions and feelings ride on another person; no one is capable of bearing that load. He or she will always let you down. Rather, you need to be a happy person in your own right, before a boyfriend or girlfriend becomes a part of your life. Making a relationship work takes a lot of work. It's not always a fun and easy process.

Even in marriage, you won't be able to depend on your spouse for your happiness. That's why it's important to learn now to be a happy person, whether or not you have a "significant other." Actually, the happier you are without a boyfriend or girlfriend, the more likely you are to get one. Happiness attracts!

Did we hit on your reason for wanting a boyfriend or girlfriend? Don't misunderstand; we're not saying that it's wrong to have or to want a "special someone" in your life. The truth is, most of us have had one or more of these five thoughts as we've contemplated having a relationship with someone of the opposite sex. But here's what we *are* saying: in order to be positive teens, we need to examine our motives and recognize that dating relationships may not be as glorious as they seem. We need to find our main source of security, identity, and happiness in our relationship with Christ. When we do, all of our other relationships will fall into place.

Radical Date Ideas

Whether you are hanging out with a group or just one person, we have a recommendation: don't get stuck doing the same old thing everyone else is doing. Be creative. Be daring (yet safe). Be fun. Step out of the norm. Try one of the following radical date ideas—or let them stir your imagination to come up with exciting dates of your own.

Dinner Delight: Find several interesting recipes to make a terrific meal. Make a list of the ingredients you need and go to the store together to purchase the items. Then come home and chop, dice, and bake. Enjoy eating the results!

Video Mania: Come up with a home movie idea or plan a video scavenger hunt. Make a list of hilarious things to video (like crawling through a store on your hands and knees), then go around town creating your video memory. When you are finished, come back to the house, pop some popcorn, and watch the finished product together.

Car Wash Date: Do something productive and hand-wash your car—or your parents' car.

Sporting Goods Fun: Do a sports activity together. You don't have to be great at the sport; in fact, sometimes it's more fun to try something new. Go bowling or skeet shooting. Play tennis. Hit golf balls. Try paint ball, go-carts, or ice skating.

Shop till You Drop: Shopping can be fun if you go to stores that you can enjoy together. Bookstores, sports stores, toy stores, and electronics stores can be great. Go with a purpose in mind (say, shopping for a gift for someone or catching a sale). Make a game of shopping by deciding on an amount to spend (maybe five or ten dollars) and have a contest to see who can get the most for their money. Don't forget to check out local flea markets and garage sales too.

The Great Outdoors: Pack a picnic lunch, go on a hike together, play Frisbee in the park, or walk the dog and enjoy the beautiful weather. Consider stargazing at night, with or without a telescope.

The Big Event: Keep an eye out for local concerts, fairs, or festivals in your area. Make fond memories by attending a special event together.

Water Balloon Fight: Fill a cooler full of water balloons, then go to a park or open field and have at it. Try tossing the balloons back and forth, taking a step farther away from each other with every throw. See how far you can chuck the balloon before it bursts.

Work It Out: If you are the athletic sort, consider working out together. Running, lifting weights, swimming, or bicycling together can each make a great date (and have positive results for your health!).

Creative Collaboration: Choose a craft that you and your friend (or friends) would enjoy and expend some creative energy together. Walk through a craft store to get ideas. If you are musically oriented, create a song together and record it.

Charity Work: What opportunities for service can be found in your community? As a couple or a group, you might want to get involved with Meals on Wheels, Special Olympics, or the local homeless shelter. Contact your church missions department or community center to find out where help is needed.

Prayer Date: Visit some of your town's churches and chapels together. We don't mean during regular service hours on Sunday morning or Wednesday night (although those can be good date times too); we mean during off hours, when the church or chapel doors are open for people to come in and pray. When Mom and Dad were dating as students at Baylor University, they visited some local chapels just to read Scripture and pray together. Dad asked Mom to marry him on one of those visits. He memorized 1 Corinthians 13—the entire chapter!— and recited it to her. (Now there's an idea, guys!)

Best Burger Hunt: Try out different local hamburger joints to determine which one has the best burgers in town. Don't forget to try some of those hole-in-the-wall places; sometimes the dives have the best burgers and fries. After you find the best burger, the hunt is on to find the best milkshake in town!

Playing It Safe

If we play too close to the fire, we're going to get burned; and if we flirt with temptation, we're likely to succumb. So when it comes to dating—and the sexual temptation that often goes with it—we need to play it safe by defining certain personal rules for ourselves.

Scripture warns us quite clearly to run, flee, and hightail it away from the opportunity for sexual sin. Proverbs 4:25–27 says, "Look straight ahead, and fix your eyes on what lies before you. Mark out a straight path for your feet; then stick to the path and stay safe. Don't get sidetracked; keep your feet from following evil." Solomon goes on to talk about the dangers of getting caught in the trap of sexual immorality, and he warns his readers to run from people who are immoral. Finally, he sums up his message by describing the fate of a person who falls into sexual temptation: "He will die for lack of self-control; he will be lost because of his incredible folly" (Proverbs 5:23).

Often the difference between a wise person and a foolish one is that the wise person makes a plan to steer clear of temptation. Temptation will always be there; it's a reality of life. But a wise person guards himself or herself from getting too close to it. In the Old Testament, for example, Joseph fled from Potiphar's wife when she invited him to sleep with her. He didn't stay around to think about it, as you can read in Genesis 39:6–12. Paul gives the ultimate warning about the dangers of sexual sin in 1 Corinthians 6:18–20:

> Run away from sexual sin! No other sin so clearly affects the body as this one does. For sexual immorality is a sin against your own body. Or don't you know that your body is the temple of the

May the grace of our Lord Jesus Christ, the love of God, and the fellowship of the Holy Spirit be with you all. —2 Corinthians 13:13

Holy Spirit, who lives in you and was given to you by God? You do not belong to yourself, for God bought you with a high price. So you must honor God with your body.

So what are some prudent measures to keep ourselves safe and free from sin in this important area of our lives? Here are some personal rules for dating that we recommend:

- No one of the opposite sex allowed in your bedroom
- No hanging out at home together when no one else is around
- No lying down on the couch kissing
- No parking and getting in the backseat together
- No touching of any areas that would be covered by (modest) bathing suits

You may come up with other rules to add to this list. The important thing is to set your boundaries *before* you begin dating. Decide in your heart and mind what you are and are not willing to do in a dating relationship. Knowing your limits beforehand will help you put on the brakes if your passion starts to take over in a certain situation. It will keep you from getting too close to temptation and possibly falling into temptation without meaning to.

Other than the general rules we listed, we're not going to try to tell you exactly what your boundaries ought to be. But we will say that the wisest, most positive thing you can do is to save most of your physical affection for your marriage relationship. When it comes to your body and your heart, be careful what you give. As Justin Lookadoo and Hayley Morgan put it in their book, *Dateable,* "How much you put in determines how much it will hurt when it ends!"[1]

Marilyn Morris speaks to teens across the nation about the

importance and the benefits of abstinence. We think what she says in her program, "Aim for Success," makes a lot of sense. See what you think:

When you meet someone, there's a natural progression that takes place. It starts with talking and can go all the way down to having sexual intercourse:

Talking

A hug and kiss

Kissing passionately

Touching under clothes

Removing your clothes

Having sexual intercourse

It's your job to determine where you are going to stop. Teens often think that if they stop right before they go all the way, they will be safe, but a person can get sexually transmitted diseases by going that far.

I've talked to college students and asked where they would recommend middle school and high school-aged students stop if they're serious about their dreams and goals and serious about avoiding pregnancies, STDs, and emotional scars. College students have told me teenagers should consider stopping somewhere between talking to each other and a quick kiss and hug. When I ask them why, they are quick to tell me that when a person gets involved in hot, heavy, passionate kissing, they are going to get really turned on. And when a person is turned on, it's difficult to turn off, making it very easy to slide down that progressive slope, even though the person said he or she was committed to abstinence. So the question is, where do you plan to stop to make sure you get to fulfill your dreams and goals and protect yourself from pregnancies, STDs, and emotional scars?[2]

The Gift of Purity

We like to look at abstinence this way. Think about the nicest gift you have ever given someone. Maybe it was a Mother's Day gift to your mom or a birthday gift to your best friend. Giving precious and treasured gifts is not only a blessing to the recipient but also to the giver!

Now think about the lifelong partner you will have one day. Possibly the best gift you can give that person is a gift you can start preparing now, before you've even met: the gift of sexual purity.

We know, the media makes it seem as if maintaining your virginity is ridiculous and impossible. But TV, movies, and magazines don't tell the whole truth. Actually, it does take a strong person—a person of principle, character, and self-control—to stay pure until marriage. And by God's grace, there are many such people! The Hollywood scene doesn't speak for all of us. The sad truth is that immorality in the teenage years can bring heartache into a marriage, while "saving yourself" for your spouse can reap untold blessings. Hollywood doesn't tell that side of the story.

Take Jenny (not her real name), for instance. She led a wild life in high school and college, sleeping around with her steady boyfriend and later with many others. By God's grace she came to know Christ after she graduated from college. God also brought a wonderful Christian man into her life, and eventually they got married. Unfortunately, the consequences of a sinful lifestyle don't evaporate when someone becomes a Christian. Because of one of her college encounters, Jenny had a sexually transmitted disease (STD). Not only did she give the

STD to her husband, but she experienced extreme pain whenever they had intercourse. After years of counseling and trips to the doctor, their marriage is surviving; but Jenny would tell you, it has been an unpleasant road to take.

STDs are rampant in our culture. Of course, no one talks about them. You don't see the latest movie stars mentioning them, or the wild girls in the senior class talking about them, but they're there. Sometimes an STD lies dormant in a carrier for years before it is detected. A person can be harboring an STD without knowing it, giving it as an inadvertent "gift" to every new sexual partner.

There is only one sure way to prevent STDs: keeping yourself pure for your marriage partner. It's that clear—as are God's rules about avoiding sexual immorality. It's a shame so many people think that living outside of God's rules is the fun way to do life. Ultimately, living outside of God's plan only leads to heartache, frustration, guilt, and despair.

Don't believe the media hype. Sexual purity *is* possible. Premarital sex *isn't* okay. And don't fall for the big Condom Lie. Many teenagers think, *As long as we use a condom, we'll be okay.* Ask any married couple who is trying to not get pregnant: are condoms their preferred method of birth control? OK, don't ask them; that would be embarrassing. We'll tell you the answer: no! Married couples who aren't ready to have children know that condoms are unreliable. They tear, they leak—they're the most unreliable form of birth control available.

So why does our culture push condoms? Because people are reaching for ways to say it's OK to lead a sinful lifestyle with no consequences. Don't buy into the lie! The only safe sex is the best sex: the kind that's saved for marriage.

Dating, after all, is merely a preparation for marriage. Why waste ourselves on practice, when we can save ourselves for the real deal? This isn't reality TV; this is reality! By approaching dating not as a game, but as a training ground for life, we truly become positive teens.

POWER POINT

⚙ **Read:** Ephesians 5:25–33. What is marriage a picture of? How does knowing this help you to stay pure until marriage? Now read Ephesians 6:10–20. What weapons do Christians have to battle temptation and lead the life God intends for them?

◉ **Pray:** Great and glorious Lord, you are the lover of my soul! No one else can fill that place. Thank you for your unfailing love that is abundant and merciful toward me. I find great joy in your loving embrace. Help me to love my brothers and sisters in Christ with a pure and godly love. Keep me from being swayed by the culture and falling into temptation. Please equip me with the self-control and strength I need to stay pure until marriage. I desire to give that gift of purity to my one and only marriage partner. Thank you for giving me the power I need to carry out your plan for my life. In Jesus's name I pray, amen.

♡ **Remember:** 1 Corinthians 10:13: "But remember that the temptations that come into your life are no different from what others experience. And God is faithful. He will keep the temptation from becoming so strong that you can't stand up against it. When you are tempted, he will show you a way out so that you will not give in to it."

☺ **Do:** Spend some time in prayer, asking God what your personal boundaries and rules should be for relationships with the opposite sex. Write these rules down on a piece of paper, and write out 1 Corinthians 10:13 on the bottom of the page. Keep the page in a place where you will see it often. Next, choose one loyal friend with whom you can share your relationship goals. Talk about your personal boundaries and agree to hold one another accountable.

Power Principle #5

THe Power OF AttiTuDe

Ability is what you're capable of doing. Motivation determines what you do. Attitude determines how well you do it.

—Lou Holtz

There is little difference in people, but that little difference makes a big difference. The little difference is attitude. The big difference is whether it is positive or negative.

—Clement Stone

Having Hope
Looking Up When Everything Seems Down

So I pray that God, who gives you hope, will keep you happy and full of peace as you believe in him. May you overflow with hope through the power of the Holy Spirit.

—Romans 15:13

It's easy to have hope when things are rolling along OK in life. But what about when things go terribly wrong? When you're down in the dumps, when it seems as if your whole world is falling apart, that's when you need true hope. But how do you obtain it? Where does hope come from?

Jennifer Harmon from Orlando, Florida, knows what it's like to face tragedy in life. She also knows how to find hope in the midst of it. Mom met Jennifer several years ago through a mutual friend, and her story deeply touched Mom's heart. We'll let Jennifer share her own story:

I could have been described as a pretty normal teenager. I was always busy with school and was an active member in my high school's JROTC program. The rest of my time was spent either working at Subway or hanging out with friends. I loved running, juggling, playing guitar, going to the beach, surfing, partying, and basically anything fun.

Although I was raised in a Christian family and had to go to church almost every Sunday, I didn't believe God was real. I had everything I thought I needed in life. All my hopes and dreams were in myself and what I could accomplish. I saw life as just a fun ride to enjoy while it lasted. And being young, I thought nothing but good times, friends, dating, school, work, etc., would be in store for me. Why would I need God when I was doing fine on my own?

The summer after I graduated from high school was one of the happiest times of my life. I had just turned eighteen and was spending my last easygoing, fun-filled summer before starting college at the University of Central Florida. Everything seemed to be falling into place. It appeared as though nothing but promise lay ahead.

But all those plans took a drastic turn one hot Fourth of July afternoon. I decided to go with my friends from work to a party to celebrate the holiday. There was supposed to be skiing, volleyball, etc., but when I arrived everyone was just sitting around talking. I was bored and hot from sitting outside, so I decided to take a quick dive into the lake. I changed into my bathing suit and headed toward the dock. I had no idea I was about to dive into three feet of water.

I remember everything about the dive. I thought it was a great dive. It had great form (as weird as that may sound). But those carefree thoughts were quickly interrupted by the bottom of the shallow lake below. I remember how unexpectedly my hands touched the slimy bottom. They immediately buckled, and then my head made contact. I heard my neck snap, flipped over, and ended up facedown in the water. I knew I had to get out quickly to make sure I was OK. I tried to swim but wasn't going anywhere. The real shock came when I opened my eyes and saw my whole body floating motionlessly in the water. I couldn't move at all!

Extreme panic set in. All my concentration went to holding my breath. Since I've always been such a prankster, I knew my friends would think I was kidding. The longer I held my breath the more I

Things never go so well that one should have no fear, nor so ill that one should have no hope. —Danish proverb

felt like I was going to die. I couldn't believe my life was going to end like this! I held my breath until I couldn't hold it anymore. I remember thinking, *Well, I guess this is it.* I was just about to breathe in water when someone finally pulled me out. I've never been so relieved! They laid me down by the waterside, questioned me, and called an ambulance.

When the paramedics arrived, I was airlifted to the hospital. I couldn't believe what had happened. It didn't seem real. I couldn't move or feel anything below my shoulders! I tried to imagine spending my whole life paralyzed. Just the thought of it made me want to die right then and there.

Before my surgery my family came in to pray that everything would go smoothly. From that point I don't remember very much. I spent nine days in critical condition battling pneumonia, a collapsed lung, a staph infection, and a urinary tract infection. Things were looking pretty bad. My parents tried to remain hopeful, but every day they were told, "She's probably not going to make it."

After I was transferred to Atlanta's Shepherd Center, things started looking a little better. I remember waking up one morning in the ICU. I noticed the ventilator tube coming out of my throat. I couldn't talk; there was something stuck down my nose; and, of course, I couldn't move. Because of all the drugs I was on, it was hard to get a grip on reality at first. However, as time went on and the drugs wore off, it became more and more difficult to deal with the new circumstances of my life. I can't stress enough how much shock and disbelief I was in. My life had become a horrible dream from which I kept expecting to wake up. But this time the nightmare would not go away.

The first month was by far the most difficult for me. It seemed as if I'd had everything taken away from me. It was worse than the most extreme punishment, and it was permanent. I lost my job, car, old room, every material possession (surfboard, guitars, juggling balls, bicycle, etc.), and all of my independence.

All my hopes and dreams for my life appeared to be shattered. All my rights as a human seemed to have been taken away. I remember thinking, *Why did I try so hard in life, just for this to happen? What did I do to deserve this? Why did this happen to me?*

Another question that ran continuously through my head was, *What if?* It was like a meaningless attempt to find a way out of the disaster. What if I had done a cannonball? What if I had just left the party? What if I had never taken the job at Subway (and never met the friends I went to the party with)? The questions were endless and obviously never helped the situation.

In addition to the denial and the what ifs, the thought came to me that if there was a God, maybe he was punishing me. Or maybe he was trying to get my attention. In desperation I promised God that I would be as perfect as humanly possible if he would just give me another chance. This phase lasted only a couple of weeks. After I started adapting more to my situation, I quickly slipped back into my doubts and disbelief.

At first I completely believed that I was going to regain movement. Walking wasn't my greatest concern, but I was positive I would at least use my hands again. Perhaps I was in more denial, or perhaps this was the last glimmer of hope I had left to hold on to. I could not wait for the day that I would be able to take care of all my personal needs, play guitar, or just give someone a hug. But waiting was all I did.

Finally I had no choice but to try to accept the possibility that I may never move anything again. This was undoubtedly the hardest part I had to go through. It was incredibly depressing having to say good-bye to all I had ever known. I would stare at my old pictures all day and cry.

In the middle of physical therapy one morning, the song "Happy" by Sister Hazel came over the speaker system and filled the gym. Immediately the memories of the night before my accident flooded my mind. Everything was perfect then. I was at a Fourth of July celebration watching fireworks, listening to Sister Hazel play, hanging out with all my friends, and having a great time living a normal life.

I wanted to be that girl again. She could laugh. She knew how to have fun. She was happy. She didn't belong in a wheelchair. As the song played, I cried. I wanted my old life back. But as much as I didn't want to believe that the accident had happened, there was no way around it. I had to deal with it sooner or later.

I distinctly remember the day I started to accept my injury. It was shortly after the second month, and I was once again crying, thinking about what my life had become. Only this time I started feeling something different. I was just so sick of crying about everything. That's when it finally clicked. There was no changing what happened, so I needed to pick up whatever pieces I could and move on. I had to stop feeling sorry for myself and try to press forward the best I could.

That was the good news. The bad news was that I once again pushed the possibility of God out of my life. I wanted to prove that I could handle everything on my own. As much as possible, I wanted to be the same person I was before the accident. There was no reason to change my life for a God I couldn't see any evidence of. I didn't have any real hope for my life. Since there was no getting back the old hopes and dreams that were destroyed by my accident, all I could do was try to stay happy and busy to the best of my ability and then die.

The event that finally started changing my mind about God was the terrorist attack on September 11, 2001. I began to think about how fragile and uncertain our lives are. I started to wonder if God was real and if I should give him a chance. Could there be any evidence of his existence? What if there was an afterlife? I had to face the reality that one day I will die, and nothing in my life will matter anymore except my relationship with God.

I was finally ready to give Jesus a chance. I made the choice to constantly seek and learn more about him, and he never let me down. I was completely in awe of how true and incredible God really is. He opened my eyes and gave me a hope that is greater than anything this world can offer.

I no longer see my life as insignificant and meaningless, because I know that the God of all creation knows, loves, and cares about me. I know he has greater purposes for me than anything I can imagine. And beyond the hope of this lifetime, I have the greatest hope of spending eternity with him. No matter what difficult circumstance I am facing, I have hope, because my God is greater than my circumstances. God has given me a new life, and now I look forward to each day with new hope and with God as my best friend.[1]

Hope to You

You may not have had a life-changing experience like Jennifer's, but most likely you have (or will have) challenges, struggles, and discouragements in your lifetime. We all have them. That's why it's good to know that no matter where we are in life or what we're experiencing, one thing is for sure: God will never leave us. He is faithful. Circumstances change, and people disappoint us, but God is always there by our side. When we put our trust in him, we have reason for hope!

How do we know that God is with us? Jesus's final words to the disciples before he ascended into heaven gave them the hope they needed to carry on the gospel message. They give us hope as well: "And be sure of this: I am with you always, even to the end of the age" (Matthew 28:20). Jesus also said that God would send the Holy Spirit to be with us, teach us, empower us, and comfort us (John 16:5–15; Acts 1:8).

There is hope in the fact that God is with us, and there is hope in the fact that God has a plan for our lives. Jeremiah 29:11 says, "'For I know the plans I have for you,' says the LORD. 'They are plans for good and not for disaster, to give you a future and a hope.'" Although we may be discouraged and not understand why something has happened, God has a bigger picture in mind. He sees the eternal. While our situation may seem hopeless from our perspective, God is at work. He is not finished with us or with his plan for us.

Psalm 37:23–24 reminds us, "The steps of the godly are directed by the LORD. He delights in every detail of their lives. Though they stumble, they will not fall, for the LORD holds them by the hand." Personally, as we consider Jennifer's heartrending story, we recognize that even the parts that we don't like about life—the circumstances beyond our control—can be used by God for a greater purpose. Life is not over just because it gets difficult. Our loving Father has a plan of hope that is far greater than what we see in our present situation.

Hope from God

David, one of the most significant characters in the Old Testament, found his hope and help in God and his Word. Now, David didn't have an easy life. King Saul was so jealous of David that he tried to kill him on numerous occasions. David was forced to flee from his homeland

There is no medicine like hope, no incentive so great, and no tonic so powerful as expectation of something better tomorrow. —Orison Sweet Marden

and live in enemy territory in a foreign country. If ever there was a reason to be discouraged, David had one!

Most of us have probably never lived under an actual death threat. But all of us have experienced (or will experience) discouragement or even despair in some form or fashion. Maybe you've lost your best friend, and you feel as if you have no one to talk to anymore. Maybe your grades have dropped, and you can't seem to bring them back up. Maybe you've had to face a tough family issue, and now you're struggling with the realization that things will never be the same at home again.

If you feel discouraged, imagine how David must have felt when he was forced to flee from his best friend and his wife and live in the land of the Philistines in order to get away from Saul and his army. He must have felt completely abandoned. Consider David's cry in Psalm 42:

> As the deer pants for streams of water,
>> so I long for you, O God.
> I thirst for God, the living God.
>> When can I come and stand before him?
> Day and night, I have only tears for food,
>> while my enemies continually taunt me,
>>> saying,
> "Where is this God of yours?"
>
> My heart is breaking
>> as I remember how it used to be:
> I walked among the crowds of worshipers,
>> leading a great procession to the house of God,
> singing for joy and giving thanks—
>> it was the sound of a great celebration!

Why am I discouraged?
> Why so sad?

I will put my hope in God!
> I will praise him again—
> my Savior and my God!

Now I am deeply discouraged,
> but I will remember your kindness—

from Mount Hermon, the source of the Jordan,
> from the land of Mount Mizar.

I hear the tumult of the raging seas
> as your waves and surging tides sweep over me.

Through each day the LORD pours his unfailing love upon me,
> and through each night I sing his songs,
> praying to God who gives me life.

"O God my rock," I cry,
> "Why have you forsaken me?

Why must I wander in darkness,
> oppressed by my enemies?"

Their taunts pierce me like a fatal wound.
> They scoff, "Where is this God of yours?"

Why am I discouraged?
> Why so sad?

I will put my hope in God!
> I will praise him again—
> my Savior and my God!

Perhaps you're at the point of wanting to throw in the towel. You're crying out, "Where is God? Why did he let this happen to me?"

Both King David and Jennifer (not to mention countless others) have asked the same questions. And they found one answer. Although we can't always understand God and his ways, we can place our hope in his love and goodness. It's not our job to figure God out. We can't do it. That's the entire message of the story of Job. Things happen that are far beyond our comprehension; yet God never leaves us. He is with us, even in the midst of tragedy, struggle, and pain. He sees the bigger picture, and he has an eternal plan for our lives. We have reason to hope!

A Gift to Others

Hope makes a great gift. In fact, it is possibly one of the greatest gifts we can give to another person. You see, when people feel defeated, afraid, or discouraged, they also feel alone. They can't see beyond their situation, sadness, or pain. They need someone to remind them of God's healing hand and the hope they have in him.

We don't have to have perfect, trouble-free lives to offer hope. In fact, by going through our own tragedies or difficulties, we are often better equipped to help and encourage those who find themselves in similar situations. Notice the hope and comfort we not only receive but can also give, as described in 2 Corinthians 1:3–7:

> All praise to the God and Father of our Lord Jesus Christ. He is the source of every mercy and the God who comforts us. He comforts us in all our troubles so that we can comfort others. When others are troubled, we will be able to give them the same comfort God has given us. You can be sure that the more we suffer for Christ, the more God will shower us with his comfort through Christ. So when we are weighted down with troubles, it is for your benefit and salvation! For when God comforts us, it is so that we, in turn, can be an encouragement to you. Then you can patiently

endure the same things we suffer. We are confident that as you share in suffering, you will also share God's comfort.

Romans 10:13–15 reminds us of the greatest hope we can bring to someone else:

> For "Anyone who calls on the name of the Lord will be saved." But how can they call on him to save them unless they believe in him? And how can they believe in him if they have never heard about him? And how can they hear about him unless someone tells them? And how will anyone go and tell them without being sent? That is what the Scriptures mean when they say, "How beautiful are the feet of those who bring good news."

To be positive teens, we must be open to this possibility: we may be the messengers God wants to send to bring the good news of God's love to other teenagers who need hope! Perhaps someone we know is lonely, afraid, or discouraged. He or she may not know about the salvation and hope that's available through Jesus Christ. We can help that person cross the bridge of hope. In the process, we may find that our own sense of encouragement is strengthened. That's not our motive, of course; but a boost in our own self-esteem is often the unexpected by-product of sharing the gift of hope with others.

Could you be the one God wants to use to bring a healing message of hope to someone else? Are you open? Are you aware? Are you listening for God's "still, small voice"? (1 Kings 19:12). How wonderful to know that we can be not only the recipients of hope but the givers of hope as well!

POWER POINT

⚙ **Read:** Psalm 40. What does the psalmist say about what God has done for him? What does he ask of God? Was the psalmist's life filled with only good circumstances? Where was his hope?

⊚ **Pray:** God of hope and comfort, I praise you, for you are faithful to sustain me. You will never leave me. Thank you for your faithful love and mercy! Help me to keep my eyes on you through the difficult times. My desire is to walk with you and find my hope in you and not in other people. Lord, give me hope when I am discouraged and down. Please allow me to see that glimmer of hope when everything seems dark. I also want to keep my eyes on you during the good times in my life as well. Help me to share the hope you have given me with other people. Thank you, Lord, for both the wonderful times and the discouragements in my life, for I learn from them both. In Christ's name, amen.

♡ **Remember:** Psalm 40:11: "LORD, don't hold back your tender mercies from me. My only hope is in your unfailing love and faithfulness."

☺ **Do:** Be a messenger of hope to someone today. Do you have a friend who is down or discouraged? What can you do for that person: Call him (or her) on the phone? Write a note? Offer to go out for coffee? Extend a caring hand and an encouraging word. Assure your friend that God is still there and so are you. Share the gospel message if he or she doesn't already know Jesus.

Got Joy?
Experiencing a Real Rush

Joy is not a luxury or a mere accessory in the Christian life. It is the sign that we are really living in God's wonderful love, and that love satisfies us.

—Andrew Murray

Do you remember the ad campaign for milk that used the short phrase "Got Milk?" Those two words were accompanied by pictures of various celebrities with giant, white milk stains on their upper lips. The evidence of their love for milk showed clearly on their faces!

Now, we may not all be milk lovers, but the evidence of what we love should still show in our faces—and in all that we say and do. The question is, can others clearly see our love and thankfulness for Christ through the joy we show in our lives?

Sadly, finding a Christian who radiates joy can be like finding Waldo in one of those "Where's Waldo?" puzzles. It shouldn't be that difficult! As Christians, we should be the most joyful creatures on the face of this earth. After all, we have a God who never leaves us. We walk in his grace. We are recipients of his overflowing mercy and abundant love. Through faith in his Son, we have forgiveness of sins. Yet, for many of us, the day-to-day struggles of life, combined with a persistent love for the things of this world, seem to choke out our joy in Christ.

Whatever happens, dear brothers and sisters, may the Lord give you joy. —Philippians 3:1

Perhaps more people would be drawn to the Savior if they saw more Christians who were enjoying the wonderful spiritual blessings of a life in Christ. Perhaps you have heard of the German philosopher Friedrich Nietzsche, who struggled against Christianity. He said this about the Christians of his day: "I would believe in their salvation if they looked a little more like people who have been saved."[1] Ouch!

Not Perfect, Just Joyful

Every once in a while we do come across some truly joy-filled people. We meet quite a few in the Bible. Did these joyful people have perfect lives? Quite the contrary! Take a look at David. He was filled with joy; yet, as we discussed in the last chapter, he didn't have an easy life. The apostle Paul was another person who didn't have everything go his way. In fact he was imprisoned, beaten, and left for dead more than once. Why? Because he chose to share the good news about Jesus. Now that's just not fair! If anyone had reason to feel defeated and discouraged, Paul did. Yet he wrote one of the most positive and joyful books in the Bible—the letter to the Philippians—from his prison cell. "Always be full of joy in the Lord," he encouraged the early Christians. "I say it again—rejoice!" (Philippians 4:4).

Jesus was joyful. Yes, he became "a man of sorrows, acquainted with bitterest grief" (Isaiah 53:3) for a time, as he suffered and died for our sins on the cross. But Jesus also spoke often about joy and clearly wanted his followers to experience it. As he approached his own terrible death, listen to what he said to his disciples:

> Truly, you will weep and mourn over what is going to happen to me, but the world will rejoice. You will grieve, but your grief will suddenly turn to wonderful joy when you see me again. It will be like a woman experiencing the pains of labor. When her child is

born, her anguish gives place to joy because she has brought a new person into the world. You have sorrow now, but I will see you again; then you will rejoice, and no one can rob you of that joy. At that time you won't need to ask me for anything. The truth is, you can go directly to the Father and ask him, and he will grant your request because you use my name. You haven't done this before. Ask, using my name, and you will receive, and you will have abundant joy. (John 16:20–24)

We can experience great joy, because our sins have been forgiven through Christ's death, and we have the glorious hope and promise of eternal life through his resurrection. No one and no circumstance can take that joy away from us!

The truth is, joy is not just for people who have nice, happy lives. Some of the most joyful people you'll ever meet are ones who have been through more than their fair share of challenges. That's because joy comes from the Lord, not circumstances. *Happiness* can come and go with circumstances. You get a good grade, you do something fun with a friend, you win a game, and these things make you happy. But when things don't go well, when you get a bad grade on a test or your boyfriend or girlfriend dumps you, then you tend to be sad. Joy isn't like that. Joy doesn't come and go based on what's going on in your life. You can be sad about something in your life and yet still have joy. It's gladness and peace deep inside that lasts even through the tough times.

Joy Zappers

Unfortunately, it's easy for us to allow things in our lives to rob us of the joy that is ours in Christ. These things are like clouds that keep others from seeing the joy that really should be shining through. Let's take a look at a few of these "joy zappers" that get our eyes off the eternal picture and onto ourselves and our circumstances, keeping us from experiencing—and others from seeing—the joy that God so freely gives.

Busy Lives

Soccer, student council, cheerleading, work, church activities, service projects—there are so many wonderful things that we can do with our time! But we have to be careful not to overload our plates to the point that we become stressed out. As Mom used to say when she'd take us to a buffet, "Don't put more on your tray than you can eat."

Now there's a great life lesson! Don't put more on your schedule than you can do while still maintaining a spirit of joy. I (Grace) have been known to overload my calendar with many wonderful activities like Bible studies and church events. But instead of finding joy in these activities, I end up simply going through the motions because I'm so busy. From time to time I need to remind myself of what Solomon says in Ecclesiastes 3:1: "There is a time for everything, a season for every activity under heaven."

You don't have to do everything this year—or this semester! Instead, carefully think through what is best for your schedule, which activities make the use of your gifts and talents, and which pursuits are in line with your life purpose. Say no to things that distract you from what you need to be doing. As you do the right things and protect yourself from getting frazzled and stressed, you will find that your joy can shine through your life a little more brightly.

Sin

The world's illusion is that sin is fun and will bring you happiness and joy. But happiness that results from sin is fleeting. However, doing what is right, in living in obedience to God and his Word, results in lasting joy. In John 15 Jesus gives us God's formula for overflowing joy: "I have loved you even as the Father has loved me. Remain in my love. When you obey me, you remain in my love, just as I obey my Father and remain in his love. I have told you this so that you will be filled with my joy. Yes, your joy will overflow! I command you to love each other in the same way that I love you" (John 15:9–12).

David understood that joy could be found only by staying on God's path for his life. He proclaimed, "I take joy in doing your will, my God, for your law is written on my heart" (Psalm 40:8). In Psalm 1 he wrote:

> Oh, the joys of those
>> who do not follow the advice of the wicked,
>> or stand around with sinners,
>> or join in with scoffers.
>
> But they delight in doing everything the LORD wants;
>> day and night they think about his law.
>
> They are like trees planted along the riverbank,
>> bearing fruit each season without fail.
>
> Their leaves never wither,
>> and in all they do, they prosper.
>
> But this is not true of the wicked.
>> They are like worthless chaff, scattered by the wind.
>
> They will be condemned at the time of judgment.
>> Sinners will have no place among the godly.
>
> For the LORD watches over the path of the godly,
>> but the path of the wicked leads to destruction.

Here's a little math equation that says it all:

> A little sin will
> Add to your trouble,

Subtract from your energy,

Multiply your difficulties.[2]

Let's divide our sorrows and multiply our joy by following Christ and his ways!

Self-Centeredness

It's easy for us to get caught up in ourselves—to spend all our time thinking about what we have done, what we're doing, and what we're going to do. If we dwell too much on ourselves, however, we'll either get prideful about our successes or discouraged and depressed about our failures. Either way, that kind of self-centeredness is a real joy zapper. The Bible never encourages us to only look out for "number one." Instead, Jesus reminds us that true joy comes as we "love each other in the same way that I love you" (John 15:12). And how did Jesus show his love? By selflessly serving others. In Mark 10:43–45, he said, "Whoever wants to be a leader among you must be your servant, and whoever wants to be first must be the slave of all. For even I, the Son of man, came here not to be served but to serve others, and to give my life a ransom for many."

What can *you* do for someone else? Perhaps make a phone call, write a note, give a hug? We know from personal experience that great joy results when we get our eyes off of our own petty problems and jump in with both feet to love and serve other people. Thinking of ourselves tends to rob us of our joy, but focusing on others is a definite joy giver!

Unforgiveness

Another dark cloud that can loom in our lives, hiding our joy, is unforgiveness. Are there people in your life right now who you need to forgive? Perhaps you need to forgive your parents. Yes, they are far from perfect, and they can screw up sometimes in what they say or do. But are you willing to forgive them in your heart? Maybe a friend or sibling has hurt you. He or she may not deserve forgiveness; but then, for that matter, who does? Not us! God extends his wonderful, warm hand of forgiveness to us, even though we are ugly and covered with sin. Through Christ's death on the cross, our sins have been wiped clean. Now we, too, must extend that hand of forgiveness.

Both Jesus and Paul spoke often on the topic of forgiveness. In Ephesians 4:32 Paul wrote, "Be kind to each other, tenderhearted, forgiving one another, just as God through Christ has forgiven you." In Matthew 18, Jesus told his disciples that we are to forgive our brothers and sisters not just seven times, but seventy times seven times! He went on to tell a parable about a servant who was forgiven a great debt yet would not forgive someone else who owed him a small debt. May we never be like that servant!

Worry

One of the biggest clouds that can hide our joy has nothing to do with circumstances, but rather, possibilities. Worry is a joy destroyer that can easily consume our thoughts and feelings. It's not something bad that has happened; it's only speculation and dread about what *might* happen. We can't live in the state of worry and have joy at the same time. Instead, we have to take our worries to the one who knows the future and can carry the load for us. As 1 Peter 5:7 reminds us, "Give all your worries and cares to God, for he cares about what happens to you."

We all could use a healthy diet of worrying less and praying more. To tell you the truth, we have both experienced long-term and short-term worry at times. It's easy to worry about the future. *(What if I don't do well on my SAT? What if I don't get into the college I want to go to?*

Oh, the joys of those who trust the LORD! —Psalm 40:4

163

What if I can't find the right career?) Then there are the daily, present-tense worries about schoolwork, friends, and relationships. We are beginning to learn, however, that as we deliver our cares over to God, we will see his hand at work in our lives. Let's not carry burdens that distract us and weigh us down from the plan God has for us! Instead, let's be positive teens who walk in God's joy and who choose, moment by moment, to give our cares to Christ.

Shining for Him

It's a common saying that the greatest advertisement for Christianity is a joyous Christian. Jesus said in his Sermon on the Mount, "You are the light of the world—like a city on a mountain glowing in the night for all to see. Don't hide your light under a basket! Instead, put it on a stand and let it shine for all. In the same way, let your good deeds shine out for all to see, so that everyone will praise your heavenly Father" (Matthew 5:14–16). Our joy is a light that can shine for the entire world to see. As our friends, classmates, teachers, and others see our joy in the Lord, they can't help but be drawn to God's light shining through us, or at least aroused to ask questions.

We can't produce our own joy. We can try—but true and lasting joy only comes through a relationship with Jesus Christ, as a gift from God and a fruit of his Spirit at work in us. It begins by trusting Christ through faith and becoming his follower. *Salvation* brings joy. As Paul wrote, "Oh, what joy for those whose disobedience is forgiven, whose sins are put out of sight. Yes, what joy for those whose sin is no longer counted against them by the Lord" (Romans 4:7–8).

Have you experienced the joy of having your sins forgiven? If you have never taken the opportunity to trust in God's saving grace through Jesus, please consider it today. Ephesians 2:8–9 (NKJV) says, "For by grace you have been saved through faith, and that not of yourselves; it is the gift of God, not of works, lest anyone should boast." We can't save ourselves, but God can. As we trust in the sacrifice of his Son, Jesus, for our sins, we are forgiven and become a new creation.

Joy also comes as we worship him. Psalm 100:1–2 says, "Shout with joy to the LORD, O earth! Worship the LORD with gladness. Come before him, singing with joy." Do you lack joy? Spend some time worshiping God. It will change your perspective and get your eyes off yourself and on the great God and Creator of the universe. Rejoice that he loves you, cares for you, forgives you, and accepts you as his own dear child!

Go ahead, let loose and let your joy shine brightly! That's a surefire way to become a positive teen. We close this chapter with Psalm 98:4–6, a wonderful song of worship and joy:

Shout to the LORD, all the earth;
>   break out in praise and sing for joy!
Sing your praise to the LORD with the harp,
>   with the harp and melodious song,
>   with trumpets and the sound of the ram's horn.
Make a joyful symphony before the LORD, the King!

POWER POINT

⚙ **Read:** Philippians 4 (the whole chapter). When should you have joy? What was Paul's key for being content in every circumstance?

⚙ **Pray:** Lord of heaven and earth, I praise you, for you are an awesome and wonderful God. You are my light and my salvation. In you I find joy! Thank you for forgiving me of my sins. Thank you for the promise of eternal life. Thank you for loving me and caring for me. I want to shine for you. Help others to see the joy you have given me, and may they be drawn closer to you as a result. Show me those things in my life that tend to rob me of the joy you want me to experience.

Give me your joy, peace, gladness, and contentment, even in the difficult times of my life. In Jesus' name I pray, amen.

💡 **Remember:** Philippians 4:4: "Always be full of joy in the Lord. I say it again—rejoice!"

😊 **Do:** Make a "Joy List." In a journal or on a piece of notebook paper, make a list of reasons why you can be joyful in the Lord. On the back of the page, write down some of the things that seem to be zapping your joy at this point in your life. Next to each joy zapper, write down something you can begin doing today to eliminate it. Make a decision to start fully experiencing the joy you have in Christ. See if others notice the difference!

Power Principle #6

THe Power oF Faith

Faith may be simple, but its effect is sublime.

—J. Charles Stern

*But the Lord is faithful; he will make you strong
and guard you from the evil one.
And we are confident in the Lord that you are practicing
the things we commanded you, and that you always will.
May the Lord bring you into an ever deeper understanding
of the love of God and the endurance that comes from Christ.*

—2 Thessalonians 3:3–5

Divine Communication
How to Have an Intimate Prayer Life

Don't worry about anything; instead, pray about everything.
Tell God what you need and thank him for all he has done.

—Philippians 4:6

When was the last time you communicated with one of your close friends? Was it yesterday, or perhaps a few hours ago, or even just a few minutes ago? Thanks to technology, we are never too far away from our good friends. Whether it's e-mailing, text messaging, or calling on a cell phone, communication is the key to keeping relationships alive. A friendship (including a dating relationship) soon becomes dull and lifeless if we do not converse in some form or fashion.

Fortunately, chatting with people is typically a pleasant thing—unless you're being forced to talk to your great-grandfather, who can barely hear and with whom you have virtually nothing in common. That's how some of us picture prayer: a forced attempt at communication with a big, grandfatherly God "up there" who doesn't really understand us. Nothing could be further from the truth! Prayer is meant to be a delightful conversation between a loving Father God and his precious children (that's us). If given a chance, prayer can become such a living and vibrant part of our lives that we may never want to face a day without it.

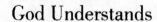

God Understands

It's hard to fathom that a perfect, eternal God would understand us and our weaknesses and problems, but he does! How? He sent his Son to live among us and to experience life as we do. Listen to the writer of Hebrews as he describes Jesus as our great High Priest (someone chosen by God to represent humans in their dealings with God):

> That is why we have a great High Priest who has gone to heaven, Jesus the Son of God. Let us cling to him and never stop trusting him. This High Priest of ours understands our weaknesses, for he faced all of the same temptations we do, yet he did not sin. So let us come boldly to the throne of our gracious God. There we will receive his mercy, and we will find grace to help us when we need it. (4:14–16)

We can pick up two wonderful truths from this passage: Jesus understands us, and he wants us to come boldly before his throne in prayer. During his time on earth, Jesus knew what it was like to be tempted; he knew persecution; he knew what it was like to be physically exhausted. We have a God who understands us! And because we do, we can trust him to care for us gently and lovingly. We can cast all our cares upon him. As 2 Peter 5:7 says, "Give all your worries and cares to God, for he cares about what happens to you."

Fellowshiping with God

Imagine that you receive a call one day inviting you to the Oval Office in the White House for a chat with the president. You are told that the president wants to build a friendship with you, so that you can communicate back and forth about important matters of state. (OK, OK—we know this is a stretch, but humor us.) For your first meeting, you plan to let the president know your viewpoints on several issues

Prayer should be the key of the day and the lock of the night. —Thomas Fuller

and ask for his assistance in those matters. How would you approach him? Would you walk right in and begin rattling off everything you want to see done during his tenure in office? Highly unlikely!

You would probably begin by thanking him for the invitation to the White House and telling him what an honor it is to meet with him. You would listen to him and get to know him before you start making requests. Even then you would probably share your requests in a humble way, knowing that the president's responses would be totally up to his own discretion.

Now imagine that the High King of heaven, the God of the universe, has invited you into his throne room. He wants to develop a friendship with you, and he wants to hear your requests. Believe it or not, this scenario is not as far-fetched as the previous one. According to Scripture, it's reality! How would you approach this benevolent King? Would you say, "Dear God, please give me a date to homecoming. I'd really like to go with someone good-looking, if you can arrange it. And could you do something to get my parents to lighten up on me? Oh yeah—I need help on my math test too. Help me to study all the right stuff, and help me to make an A. Amen"?

That kind of prayer *does* fall into the category of giving all our worries and cares to God. But if we know enough to approach the president of the United States with humility, awe, and respect, then surely we should honor and worship the God of the universe and fellowship with him before we start bombarding him with requests! Have you ever considered how wonderful it is that the God of all creation wants to have a relationship with us? How glorious it is to talk with him, to praise him for who he is, and to thank him for what he has done!

Maybe prayer is something new for you. *How do I praise and thank God?* you may be wondering. It's easier than you might think. Start by praising God for his attributes. He is all-knowing, ever-present, all-powerful, and full of mercy, kindness, and grace toward us. He is the Creator of the universe, the High King of heaven, and the lover of our souls. Jesus is the Prince of Peace, the Lamb of God, the Savior of the world. The Holy Spirit is our comforter, healer, and counselor.

Next, thank God for the blessings he has showered on you. Thank him for the people he has brought into your life. Thank him for the food on your table and the roof over your head at night. Thank him for providing for you and caring for you and hearing and answering your prayers. Thank him for his mercy and forgiveness. Thank him for being with you through the difficult times in your life.

As prayer becomes more than just an asking session, you will experience an ever-deepening fellowship with God. You'll begin to love him for who he is and not just what he can give you. Prayer will become a joy, not an obligation. We have found this to be true in our own lives. It can be true in yours as well.

What about Unanswered Prayers?

Have you ever questioned why some of your prayers aren't answered? After all, the Bible *does* say, "Ask and it will be given to you" (Matthew 7:7). Perhaps you've had the experience of pleading with God and receiving no response—or making a request and not getting the thing you asked for. Personally, we've experienced both. Waiting for God to do something with our problems can be an agonizing process!

But think about it for a minute. What are the possible answers to a request—any request? Let's say you ask your parents if you can have a television in your bedroom. Your parents have three possible responses. The first is "yes." (That would be nice and what you were hoping for.) The second is "no." (They may have specific reasons why they believe a TV in your room would not be in your best interest.) The third response is, "Let's wait awhile." (For some unknown reason, they may think you need time to mature and grow as a person before you can earn the right to have a television in your bedroom). Whatever your parents' response, it *is* an answer. It may not be what you want to hear; but then, sometimes you just have to trust that your parents love you and know what's best for you.

What if God answered "yes" to every single one of our prayers? Our world would be a scary place, because God wouldn't be in charge; *we* would! Do we really want to be the ones calling the shots, given our weaknesses, crazy ideas, and penchant for mistakes? Personally, we're thankful that God is the one in charge. He sees the big picture—the eternal one. We may think that we know what's best, but our wise and loving heavenly Father *really* knows.

Here's an example. There was a time when I (Grace) really wanted to be a singer. I even entered a competition, hoping that winning would open up new singing opportunities. I earnestly prayed that the Lord would grant me favor with the judges, but in the end I didn't get a great score. In fact the score I received was very discouraging. Yet God used this closed door to open up other areas of interest for me. I can look back now in thankfulness that God steered me in a new direction, using a "no" answer to direct me there.

If God were a "sugar daddy" who always gave us everything we wanted, would we really love him for who he is, or would we love him simply because of what he is able to give us? Thank the Lord that in his timing, he provides what we need! And thank him that he has our best interests in mind and doesn't give us everything we think we want!

Maybe you're wondering at this point, *So why do I need to ask for anything in prayer, if God already has everything planned out and knows what is best for me? Can I change the mind of God?* Well, one thing we know for certain is that God tells us to ask. Over and over again in the Bible, we find that the truly great men and women of God were praying people. Abraham, Moses, Joshua, Deborah, David, Solomon, Daniel, and all of the prophets are examples in the Old Testament. In the New Testament, when the disciples asked Jesus to teach them to pray, Jesus didn't respond, "Oh don't bother praying. God already knows your needs." Quite the contrary, he gave the disciples the great model prayer we've come to know as the Lord's Prayer (Matthew 6:9–13).

Jesus not only taught his disciples how to pray, he also told them to persevere in prayer. In Luke 18:1–8 we read the parable of the persistent widow:

> One day Jesus told his disciples a story to illustrate their need for constant prayer and to show them that they must never give up. "There was a judge in a certain city," he said, "who was a godless man with great contempt for everyone. A widow of the city came to him repeatedly, appealing for justice against someone who had harmed her. The judge ignored her for a while, but eventually she wore him out. 'I fear neither God nor man,' he said to himself, 'but this woman is driving me crazy. I'm going to see that she gets justice, because she is wearing me out with her constant requests!'"
>
> Then the Lord said, "Learn a lesson from this evil judge. Even he rendered a just decision in the end, so don't you think God will surely give justice to his chosen people who plead with him day and night? Will he keep putting them off? I tell you, he will grant justice to them quickly! But when I, the Son of Man, return, how many will I find who have faith?"

There you have it from God's own Son: we are to pray, and pray persistently. Prayer is obedience. And it changes things! Our prayers have power—not only to impact circumstances, but also to do a good work in us. Prayer keeps our eyes focused on God and his eternal plan and relieves us of worry in the present. It helps us recognize that God is in control and that we don't have to try to control things ourselves. Prayer also allows us to praise God for the good things that happen in our lives, so we don't take credit ourselves.

What Hinders Us?

Can certain things hinder our prayers from being heard? Absolutely. Take a look at Luke 18:9–14:

> Then Jesus told this story to some who had great self-confidence and scorned everyone else: "Two men went to the Temple to pray. One was a Pharisee, and the other was a dishonest tax collector. The proud Pharisee stood by himself and prayed this prayer: 'I thank you, God, that I am not a sinner like everyone else, especially like that tax collector over there! For I never cheat, I don't sin, I don't commit adultery, I fast twice a week, and I give you a tenth of my income.'
>
> "But the tax collector stood at a distance and dared not even lift his eyes to heaven as he prayed. Instead, he beat his chest in sorrow, saying, 'O God, be merciful to me, for I am a sinner.'
>
> "I tell you, this sinner, not the Pharisee, returned home justified before God. For the proud will be humbled, but the humble will be honored."

Let's take a lesson! When we come before God, we need to do so humbly, not pridefully. Our attitude should be, "Lord, may your will be done in my life. I recognize that I sin and fall short all the time. Thank you for forgiving me and for still using a sinner like me."

Of course, this parable isn't saying that it's a good thing to be a sinner. Living in disobedience to God can also be a hindrance to prayer. The psalmist said, "If I regard iniquity in my heart, the Lord will not hear me" (Psalm 66:18 AMP). Solomon said in Proverbs 28:9, "The prayers of a person who ignores the law are despised." And Jesus said, "You did not choose me, but I chose you and appointed you to go and bear fruit—fruit that will last. *Then* the Father will give you whatever you ask in my name" (John 15:16 NIV, emphasis added).

Deliberate, continual disobedience and unfruitful Christian living *will* have an impact on our prayers. Not that we have to perform a certain way in order to get God to hear us. It's wrong to think, *If I'm good enough, God will answer my prayers the way I want him to.* At the same time, Scripture is clear that if we are living in sin, our prayers may go unanswered. And remember, even if we are being "good," sometimes the most loving thing God can do is to *not* give us exactly what we want!

Another thing that can hinder our prayers is asking with our own selfish motives in mind. Listen to James's admonition to the early Christians:

> What is causing the quarrels and fights among you? Isn't it the whole army of evil desires at war within you? You want what you don't have, so you scheme and kill to get it. You are jealous for what others have, and you can't possess it, so you fight and quarrel to take it away from them. And yet the reason you don't have what you want is that you don't ask God for it. And even when you do ask, you don't get it because your whole motive is wrong—you want only what will give you pleasure. (James 4:1–3)

James put it pretty plainly, didn't he? When we pray, we need to reflect on what we are asking for, and consider whether or not we're asking with selfish motives. It all goes back to humility. We need to approach God as Jesus did when he said, "Yet I want your will, not mine" (Matthew 26:39). Are we willing to leave our requests in his hands? He knows best!

A Time and a Place

Our dog, Bear, has a favorite spot in our house where he likes to camp out. It's no small space, because Bear is no small dog. Bear is a Great Pyrenees—a giant, white, fluffy canine that's bigger than the both of us. So when Bear chooses a spot, it becomes his spot. Every day he lies at his post by the front window and watches the world go by. He's never as content as when he is sprawled out in his place.

When it comes to prayer, you need to find a good spot—a place that you can call your own. It needs to be a quiet place where you can be by yourself and commune with God. Perhaps your room is a good place (unless you share it with brothers or sisters). You know where our mom's special place was when she was growing up? Her bedroom closet. She took the phrase "prayer closet" literally! Mom grew up in Texas, and everything in Texas is big, including the closets. When Mom wanted to be alone with God, she went into her prayer closet. Her parents knew that if they hadn't seen her in a while, they could always find her there.

Many times I (Joy) enjoy going to a park near our house to have my quiet time. It's awesome to get away from everyone and focus on God and his Word in the beauty of his creation. Grace, meanwhile, enjoys seeking God in the quiet of her own room early in the morning, usually before anyone else is awake. She also likes to read the Bible and pray just before she goes to sleep.

Once you find a good place to have consistent time alone with God, the next thing to do is consider *when* you will meet with God to pray. Jesus had a good idea. In Mark 1:35 we read, "Jesus awoke long before daybreak and went out alone into the wilderness to pray." If

Time spent in prayer is never wasted. —François Fénelon

Jesus needed to spend time in prayer, don't you think that we do too? And early does seem to be a good time. Personally, we've found that beginning our day with prayer sets us off on the right foot. As we fellowship with God and turn our eyes to the eternal, the worries and cares of the day seem a little smaller, and everything seems to fall into the right place.

Why should we set a time and a place to consistently meet with God each day? It's human nature (and definitely teen nature): if we figure we'll just haphazardly meet with God whenever we feel like it, we're not likely to have much fellowship with him. Don't get us wrong; we're not saying you should be legalistic about prayer. We're simply suggesting a plan to help you keep your prayer life strong. As we look back over our own lives, we realize that the times we've been most diligent in prayer have been the times we've felt closest to God and most effective spiritually.

So keep on seeking, keep on knocking, keep on praying! An intimate prayer life is a key characteristic of a positive teen—and the key to a deep, fulfilling, and meaningful relationship with God.

POWER POINT

Read: Matthew 6:5–15 and 7:7–11. What do you learn about prayer from these passages? Can you think of a time when you experienced an answer to prayer? Is there an area of your life that you haven't turned over to the Lord in prayer?

Pray: Wonderful, loving heavenly Father, you are my creator, my healer, my deliverer, and my friend. I praise you that you have the power to do all things! Thank you for wanting to hear my prayer requests. I know you will answer according to your wisdom and in your timing. Help me to be patient. Replace my worry with peace, as I place my cares at your feet. Most importantly, grant me the ability to walk in your ways and honor you in all that I do. In Jesus's name I pray, amen.

💡 **Remember:** Philippians 4:6: "Don't worry about anything; instead, pray about everything. Tell God what you need and thank him for all he has done."

😊 **Do:** Choose a place and time for meeting with God each day. Write it in your journal or day planner. If you've picked a time in the early morning, go set your alarm clock and determine right now that you won't hit the snooze button. (OK, maybe just once.) Be committed to your precious time with God, and watch how your relationship with your heavenly Father grows and develops.

A Spiritual Sensation
Getting to Know God's Truth

For the word of God is full of living power. It is sharper
than the sharpest knife, cutting deep into our innermost
thoughts and desires. It exposes us for what we really are.

—Hebrews 4:12

Y ou've got mail!"

Who doesn't like to get mail? Whether it's e-mail or snail mail, we get a warm feeling inside when we get a message from someone we care about. Of course we usually have to wade through a lot of junk mail in order to get to the personal mail, but it's worth the effort to get to the good stuff.

Can you imagine ignoring mail from a boyfriend or girlfriend you really cared about? No way! Usually when you receive an e-mail or letter from that special someone, you go directly to it and open it first, don't you? Who in their right mind would ignore a love letter?

Actually a lot of people do—and you may be one of them. What are we talking about? We are talking about the greatest love letter ever written, addressed to each one of us, just waiting to be read. Yes, we are talking about God's love letter to us: the Bible. Isn't it peculiar how so many people (including many Christians) toss the Bible aside like junk mail?

A Treasure Book

Perhaps if we recognized the Bible for what it really is, we would hunger and thirst for it every day. What is it? It's a unique and perfect book, filled with adventure, wisdom, encouragement, love, and guide-lines. Most importantly, it is God's Word to mankind. If the Creator of the universe wants to talk to us, shouldn't we want to listen? Hebrews 4:12 says, "For the word of God is full of living power. It is sharper than the sharpest knife, cutting deep into our innermost thought and desires. It exposes us for what we really are."

Now that's one powerful book! If you are looking for true stories of adventure with real-life heroes, you can find them in Genesis, Joshua, 1 and 2 Samuel, 1 and 2 Kings, 1 and 2 Chronicles, Jonah, Daniel—and the list goes on. If you're looking for romance, check out Song of Solomon, Esther, and Ruth. The whole Bible is filled with wisdom, but if you're looking for wisdom in a nutshell, Proverbs is a good place to start. If you want comfort and encouragement, go to Isaiah or Job or the Psalms.

To find out how to live a victorious Christian life, read the New Testament letters to the early Christians—Galatians, Ephesians, Colossians, Philippians, and the rest. To discover who Jesus is and get to know his character, read the Gospels: Matthew, Mark, Luke, and John. If you want to get a glimpse of what's to come in the future, read Revelation.

The Bible is more than a collection of stories; it's an instruction manual for life. We ignore it at our peril! Not too long ago we came across a T-shirt that said on the front, "When all else fails . . ." On the back was a picture of an open Bible and the words, ". . . read the instructions."

How often have you started playing a new board game without reading the instructions? Before long, you begin to realize that the instructions could really help you enjoy the game the way it was created to be played. God has given us an instruction manual for life; let's not make the same mistake in the big game of life by thinking we

The Word of God is perfect; it is precious and pure; it is truth itself. —Martin Luther

182

can figure everything out ourselves. Life is a lot more fun and goes a lot more smoothly when we do life according to the Creator's rules, not our own.

Where Do I Begin?

Maybe you're thinking, *OK, I'm convinced. I want to get to know God's Word. But where do I start?* There are many different ways to jump into the study of the Bible. Group study is great, without a doubt. In fact, participating in a Bible study can help you learn more, dig deeper, and benefit from other people's perspectives and applications of the Scriptures. But as wonderful as group study is, we want to encourage you to have your own private time of studying God's Word. As we've discovered, when you spend time meditating on God's Word on your own, you begin to grow in true wisdom and understanding.

Here are a few suggestions for reading and studying the Bible on your own:

1. The one-year Bible. At most Christian bookstores, you can find one-year Bibles in many different versions. Typically these Bibles divide the Scriptures into 365 daily readings. Each day includes a passage from the Old Testament, a passage from the New Testament, a psalm, and a proverb. These Bibles move you through God's Word at a fast pace; but if you keep up, you will have read through the entire Bible in one year.

2. Devotionals. A variety of devotional books has been created especially for teenagers. Look in the devotional section at your local Christian bookstore to find one that fits your needs. Most devotional guides provide a Scripture passage to read and then a commentary to think about. Some provide a place to journal your thoughts.

3. Small doses. Mom's favorite way to study God's Word is to trudge along slowly, reading short passages and examining them carefully.

Then she writes down her thoughts and personal applications in a small journal. By reading short passages and thinking through them slowly, she is able to meditate on the truth and wisdom of God's Word, roll it around in her brain, and allow it to sink in throughout the day.

4. Printed Bible study. Another method for studying God's Word on your own is to use one of the many printed Bible studies that you can find at the Christian bookstore. These study books are usually short and lead you through different scriptures that apply to a specific topic (say, joy or prayer). After you read the verses, you fill in blanks or answer questions. These studies are an enjoyable way to journey through God's Word.

Whatever method you choose, decide today to begin studying God's Word and getting to know this wonderful Creator who loves you. We promise your life will be blessed. As God told Joshua in the Old Testament, "Study this Book of the Law continually. Meditate on it day and night so you may be sure to obey all that is written in it. Only then will you succeed" (Joshua 1:8).

Tips for Memorizing God's Word

If we're going to be positive teens and take to heart God's instructions to Joshua, then we need to be meditating on God's Word day and night. That doesn't mean we have to have our noses in a Bible 24/7. But we can keep God's Word close to us day and night by memorizing it. Maybe you're thinking, *Memorize Scripture? I think I'll skip to the next section.* We understand! Memorizing Scripture is not on most people's top ten list of things they love to do. Memorizing *anything* can be painful! But it's worth the effort. Why? Because the benefits are incredible!

As we just read, Joshua was promised success if he would meditate on and obey God's Word on a regular basis. And Solomon wrote in Proverbs 3:1–2: "My child, never forget the things I have taught you.

Store my commands in your heart, for they will give you a long and satisfying life." Verse 14 continues: "For the profit of wisdom is better than silver, and her wages are better than gold." When we tuck God's wisdom in our hearts and minds, we are rich indeed!

Memorizing scripture also keeps us out of trouble and helps us fight against temptation. "How can a young person stay pure?" the psalmist asks in Psalm 119:9–11. "By obeying your word and following its rules. . . . I have hidden your word in my heart, that I might not sin against you." Jesus used Scripture to fight the temptations that Satan threw at him in the wilderness (Matthew 4). And in Ephesians 6:13–18, Paul lists a number of defensive weapons we can use in the spiritual battles we face every day; but he mentions only one offensive weapon: the "sword of the Spirit, which is the word of God" (v. 17).

If we're going to be positive teens, we need to make sure we're equipped with God's wisdom wherever we go—whether it's to school, a job, a friend's house, or soccer practice. Let's not leave that wisdom at home, sitting on a coffee table. Rather, let's fill our memory banks with the wisdom God gives us in his Word. And yes, you do have the brain capacity to do it—you just need to be determined, committed, and a little bit disciplined. But the truth is, memorizing scripture really isn't that hard. We've discovered an easy and effective way to do it. It involves three steps:

1. Choose it. There is no perfect way to choose the verse you're going to memorize. You may want to choose a verse that jumped out at you during a Bible study or personal devotional time. You may want to choose one that applies to something you're going through right now. Here are some possible topics and verses:

- Salvation: Romans 3:23; 6:23; John 3:16; Ephesians 2:8–9
- Peace and contentment: Isaiah 26:3; Philippians 4:10–14

- Casting your cares on God: 2 Peter 5:7; Philippians 4:6–7
- Forgiving others: Colossians 3:13; Ephesians 4:32
- God's love: Romans 8:38–39; 1 John 4:9–10

If you get brave, you may want to memorize whole chapters of the Bible. Good ones to consider are John 15, Romans 12, Colossians 3, and Philippians 4.

2. Write it. One of the best ways to get to know a memory verse is to hand-write it five or six times or more. Use index cards or a sheet of blank business cards from an office supply store. Sometimes writing the verse in a creative way can help you remember it. For instance:

–Proverbs 13:9:

The life of the godly
Is FULL
Of light and joy ,

But the sinner's light is snuffed out.

Say the verse aloud as you write it, concentrating on the words and the reference.

3. Display it. Place your memory-verse cards in places where you are sure to see them—on your bathroom mirror or the dashboard of your car, in the kitchen, in your notebook. Display them as a way to jog your memory, but don't read them word-for-word, or these cards will become a crutch.

4. Speak it. Find one person during the week with whom you can share your verse. Say, "I'm memorizing a verse, and I need to practice it. May I say it to you?" Or, "Here's a verse I just memorized that I think may be an encouragement to you." Looking for an opportunity during the week to speak the verse to another person helps solidify it even more in your mind. You may even want to work together with a friend on memorizing verses and saying them to one another each week.

Stay diligent, and don't give up! We promise you will begin to see the benefit of memorizing scripture over time. At one point I (Grace) decided to memorize Isaiah 40:30–31: "Even youths will become exhausted, and young men will give up. But those who wait on the LORD will find new strength. They will fly high on wings like eagles. They will run and not grow weary. They will walk and not faint." I wrote this passage on a card and taped it to my mirror to remind me to persevere and never give up. Later in the year at track practice, I found strength in these verses. What's more, I was able to encourage my track team friends with them, because they were locked in my memory.

Trash or Truth

Are you the one who has to take out the trash in your home? You know as well as we do that if no one takes out the trash, it begins to smell—and if it's left in the house long enough, the whole house begins to stink. The frustrating thing is that the trash doesn't need to be taken out just once. No, we have to continue to take out the trash week after week. It definitely won't go out on its own! And if we happen to forget it, when we do finally take out the trash, we have to spray disinfectant to rid the air of the nasty odor.

It's funny how anxious we can be to get the trash out of the house; yet we rarely give a second thought to the trash that we put in our minds. Mind trash comes in all shapes and sizes: lies that we believe, negative thinking, worry, anger, bitterness, resentment. Too often we allow this trash to roll around in our minds and stink up our lives.

Then there are the other forms of trash that we, especially as teenagers, allow to muddy our minds. Think about the messages our

We can never exhaust all the treasure and worth that is in the Word. —Thomas Manton

brains receive each day from television, radio, books, movies, CDs. Some of the messages are good; but if we're honest, we have to admit that some of them are morally damaging, affecting our hearts and our actions in a negative way. Perhaps the most seriously damaging trash is pornography. Never let that kind of trash enter the house of your mind—not for a minute. It will only hurt you and your relationships for years to come.

The bottom line is that we have a choice: Will we feed our minds trash or truth? Proverbs 15:14 says, "A wise person is hungry for truth, while the fool feeds on trash." Is there any trash that needs to be bagged up and carted out of your life? Consider Ashley, who was bitter that her friend asked someone else to go to a particular concert. Instead of letting it go, she held on to the bitterness. Soon it began to stink up her friendship. Or consider William, who worried about getting into the right college. He let his worry overtake his mind; and instead of praying about getting into college, he fretted about it. Soon college entrance was all he talked about. You can imagine how popular he was in conversations with friends!

As we remove the trash from our lives, we need to replace it with truth. "Every word of God proves true," Proverbs 30:5 tells us. There is no greater source of truth than God's Word. It gives us an anchor in the storms of life and a moral foundation on which to build our lives. It also gives us the truth about God and the way he works in our lives. Don't settle for trash, lies, or even half-truths. Choose the Truth that is found in the greatest book the world has ever known: the Bible.

In Love with the Author

The story is told of a young lady who placed a book she had just finished reading on the drawing-room table, proclaiming that it was the dullest book she had ever read. Years later she fell in love with a young man, and they agreed to be married. One night she said to him, "I have a book in my library whose author's name, and even initials, are precisely the same as yours. Isn't that a singular coincidence?"

The young man replied, "I do not think so."

"Why not?" the girl inquired.

"For the simple reason that I wrote the book."

That very night the girl sat up until all hours reading the book once again. Oddly, this time it seemed to be the most interesting story she had ever read! The book that once seemed dull now seemed quite fascinating, because she knew and loved the author.[1]

In the same way, we are sure to become more and more fascinated by the Bible as we get to know and love the Author. And that's important, because we can't be truly positive teens unless we know and love God and his Word. It's only by meditating on Scripture and applying its truth daily that we can build successful, positive, and fulfilling lives.

POWER POINT

Read: Psalm 119:1–40, 89–104. What are some of the benefits of meditating on God's Word? How has the Bible benefited your life personally?

Pray: Glorious and wise heavenly Father, I praise you for your perfect Word. I delight in your Word, for it teaches me how to live and reveals more about you to me. Thank you for giving me such a living and perfect book. Teach me from your Word. Grant me wisdom as I study it. Help me to continue to love it and live it each day. Allow me to keep its truths in my heart and mind continually, so that I may freely share it with others. In Jesus's name I pray, amen.

Remember: Psalm 119:105: "Your word is a lamp to my feet and a light to my path."

Do: Begin the habit of reading and meditating on God's Word each day. Keep a journal, recording the truths that you draw from Scripture and how those truths apply to your life. Every Sunday choose a verse to memorize for that week. Write them on note cards and stick them around the house, where you will see them often. Once you have the verse memorized, tell it to a friend.

Power Principle #7

THe Power oF CouRaGe

Courage is the ladder on which all other virtues mount.

—Clare Boothe Luce

I command you—be strong and courageous! Do not be afraid or discouraged. For the LORD your God is with you wherever you go.

—Joshua 1:9

16

Standing Up
Prevailing against the Pressure

So if you are suffering according to God's will, keep on doing what is right, and trust yourself to the God who made you, for he will never fail you.

—1 Peter 4:19

Kristi was excited about Tiffany's party on Saturday night. Tiffany was a fairly new friend, and Kristi really liked Tiffany's fun and daring personality. The party plan was to have the guys and girls over for dinner and a movie, and then the girls would spend the night. Everything was great! All the right guys were there, and the party was filled with lively conversations. After the guys left, the girls went to Tiffany's room to hang out and talk about the party. That's when Tiffany's older sister, Tina, arrived.

Tina was old enough to buy alcohol, and that's just what she did, to "add a little flair" to Tiffany's party. Their parents were asleep, so the coast was clear. Every girl at the party began opening up a can of beer— every girl except Kristi. Kristi's reputation at school was one of a leader and a strong Christian. People knew where she stood and respected her for her convictions. Most people knew and accepted the fact that Kristi didn't drink.

"Come on, Kristi. Grab a beer!" one girl urged.

"Yeah, join us, Kristi," someone else said. "Don't worry. Who's going to know? It's just us."

Courage is not simply one of the virtues, but the form of every virtue at the testing point. —C. S. Lewis

Other girls joined in and made it an issue. "What, do you think you're too good for us?" they jeered.

It was decision time. Did Kristi have the courage to stand alone? She was in the middle of a mental tug of war: her convictions (along with her reputation) on one side, and the desire to fit in with her friends on the other.

We all have times when we want to feel included and be a part of the group. Most of us don't want to be made fun of or ridiculed for being a "goody-goody." More than likely every single one of us will someday face decisions like Kristi's (if we haven't already).

Courage is what it takes to stand on our convictions. If we are living for Christ and taking a stand in the way we act and speak, then we can expect to face times of temptation when those convictions are challenged. In Kristi's case, she had the courage to stand alone as she watched her friends guzzle the beer. She also watched many of them throw up in the toilet throughout the night and actually had to help one of them get home the next morning, because her friend was too hung over to get home by herself. Kristi was glad she didn't compromise. She left the party with a much higher level of self-esteem than her foolish friends.

Ingredients for Courage

How is it that some teenagers seem to have courage while others don't? We believe that courage is actually a result of three important ingredients. Each of us has the potential to be courageous if we choose to add the following ingredients to our lives:

1. Courageous people know the difference between right and wrong. How do we know right from wrong? Remember what we learned in the last chapter? The Bible is our Creator's instruction book for life. Second Timothy 3:16 tells us that God's Word "is useful to teach us what is true and to make us realize what is wrong in our lives. It straightens us out and teaches us to do what is right." We need to know what we believe, and that belief needs to be founded on God's Word.

2. Courageous people have a deep conviction in their hearts about taking a stand for what is right. It's one thing to know what is right; it is another thing to do what is right. Psalm 119:30–31 says, "I have chosen to be faithful; I have determined to live by your laws. I cling to your decrees. LORD, don't let me be put to shame." Courage takes a personal determination to stand by what we know is right.

3. Courageous people find their strength from God. When David fought Goliath, it took a tremendous amount of courage. But David didn't act out of his own strength; instead, he relied on God's strength as he declared, "The LORD who saved me from the claws of the lion and the bear will save me from this Philistine!" (1 Samuel 17:37). Noah, Joseph, Moses, Joshua, Caleb, Job, Daniel, Paul, Stephen (and the list goes on and on) were all courageous men who found their strength not in themselves, but in the Lord.

What Convictions?

Let's examine several of the issues that we, as teenagers, may find ourselves up against during the next several years. These are areas in which we may need courage. As we consider these issues, let's also look at what the Scriptures say about them. That way we can stand firm in these areas of our lives, knowing that we are standing on the sure foundation of God's Word.

Alcohol and Drug Use

Not only is it against the law for teenagers to partake in these substances, but alcohol and drugs can also ruin our dreams in life. Some may grumble, "Oh come on, what's the harm?" Well, it's time for a reality check. When you are under the influence of drugs or alcohol, you are much more likely to give in on other areas of immorality. If you're drunk or high, you have little ability to guard yourself against temptation, especially sexual temptation. The possibilities of contracting an STD or getting pregnant do not even enter your mind when you're in such a state.

People say and do stupid things when they are under the influence of mind-altering substances. And who among us wants to be known as a "drunken idiot"? The fact is, word travels fast when you decide to participate in illegal substances, and a once-respected reputation can soon become tainted and marred. Even worse, you run the risk of becoming addicted. If that happens, you can kiss all your dreams for a positive, successful, and productive life good-bye.

In order to steer clear of these substances, you must have courage—courage to stand alone and do what is right. When others are making fun of you for drinking only a soft drink and saying, "Oh come on, just this once," courage must kick in. Be prepared ahead of time to say, "No, thank you."

Here are some scriptures to back you up:

- Proverbs 23:29–35: "Who has anguish? Who has sorrow? Who is always fighting? Who is always complaining? Who has unnecessary bruises? Who has bloodshot eyes? It is the one who spends long hours in the taverns, trying out new drinks. Don't let the sparkle and smooth taste of wine deceive you. For in the end it bites like a poisonous serpent; it stings like a viper. You will see hallucinations, and you will say crazy things. You will stagger like a sailor tossed at sea, clinging to a swaying mast. And you will say, 'They hit me, but I didn't feel it. I didn't even know it when they beat me up. When will I wake up so I can have another drink?'"

- Isaiah 5:11–12, 22: "Destruction is certain for you who get up early to begin long drinking bouts that last late into the night. You furnish lovely music and wine at your grand parties; the harps, lyres, tambourines, and flutes are superb! But you never think about the LORD or notice what he is doing. Destruction is certain for those who are heroes when it comes to drinking, who boast about all the liquor they can hold."

- Romans 13:13–14: "We should be decent and true in everything we do, so that everyone can approve of our behavior. Don't participate in wild parties and getting drunk, or in adultery and immoral living, or in fighting and jealousy. But let the Lord Jesus Christ take control of you, and don't think of ways to indulge your evil desires."

- Ephesians 5:17–18: "Don't act thoughtlessly, but try to understand what the Lord wants you to do. Don't be drunk with wine, because that will ruin your life. Instead, let the Holy Spirit fill and control you."

- 1 Thessalonians 5:5–6: "For you are all children of the light and of the day; we don't belong to darkness and night. So be on your guard, not asleep like the others. Stay alert and be sober."

A few words to the wise: your best bet is to not go to parties where you know drinking is going on, even if you're not planning to drink. Several years ago in Dallas, the police made a huge bust of hundreds of high-school kids at a keg party. All of the students (even the ones who weren't drinking) were rounded up and taken to the police station.

If you do find yourself in a party situation where there is drinking, play it safe. Some college students we know have suggested getting your own soft drink (don't let someone else get it, since it could be spiked), and holding your own cup all night. This way when someone approaches you and says, "Hey, can I get you something to drink?" you can say, "I already have something." You won't be hassled, and you can be assured that what you're drinking is nonalcoholic.

And please, don't think that you can have "just one drink" in order to fit in. Once you have one, your strength to say no to a second is reduced. Most teenagers in that situation do have another and another until they are drunk. Don't go there! Resist temptation, and don't get started with the first drink.

Sexual Immorality

"Oh come on. You're not going to stay a virgin all of your life, are you?" Ever heard that? The pervasive theme of our current culture is sex, sex, sex. Society ridicules those who choose to remain pure until marriage. In almost every movie or television show, the expected norm is to have premarital or extramarital sex.

Do you have the courage to do what is right and stay sexually pure until marriage? It takes strength and conviction to go against the tide. We already discussed this issue briefly in chapter 11; now let's examine what the Bible has to say to us on the issue:

- Exodus 20:14: "Do not commit adultery."
- Matthew 15:19–20: "For from the heart come evil thoughts, murder, adultery, all other sexual immorality, theft, lying, and slander. These are what defile you."
- 1 Timothy 1:10–11: "These laws are for people who are sexually immoral, for homosexuals and slave traders, for liars and oath breakers, and for those who do anything else that contradicts the

right teaching that comes from the glorious Good News entrusted to me by our blessed God."

- 1 Peter 4:1–5: "So then, since Christ suffered physical pain, you must arm yourselves with the same attitude he had, and be ready to suffer, too. For if you are willing to suffer for Christ, you have decided to stop sinning. And you won't spend the rest of your life chasing after evil desires, but you will be anxious to do the will of God. You have had enough in the past of the evil things that godless people enjoy—their immorality and lust, their feasting and drunkenness and wild parties, and their terrible worship of idols. Of course, your former friends are very surprised when you no longer join them in the wicked things they do, and they say evil things about you. But just remember that they will have to face God, who will judge everyone, both the living and the dead."

Cheating

You may think that everyone cheats, but the courageous do not. Those who know that cheating is wrong and stand on that conviction may end up with a lower grade; but in the long run, they will have a trusted reputation and strength of character that will take them much further than a simple grade on a test. It's not easy to follow your convictions when you forget to study and an easy way to cheat presents itself. Dishonesty is easy; honesty takes courage.

We have already discussed dishonesty in chapter 8, and you can zip back there to refresh your memory on what Proverbs has to say about the subject. You can also look up the following stories in the New Testament, which remind us that cheating is despicable to God:

- Matthew 21:12–13: Jesus clears the temple of the dishonest money changers.

The test of courage comes when we are in the minority. —Ralph W. Sockman

- Luke 19:1–10: Jesus converts Zacchaeus, the cheating tax collector.
- Acts 5:1–11: Ananias and his wife, Sapphira, are slain by the Holy Spirit for lying to God.

Irresponsibility

How many times have you heard the phrase "It's not my fault"? How many times have *you* said those words? We've said them too! Sometimes "It's not my fault" is a valid statement; but sometimes it's simply an excuse to cover up a mistake or bad decision. It takes courage to tell the truth and say, "Yes, I made a mistake," or, "Yes, it is my fault."

It takes courage to speak up, take responsibility, and tell the truth. A recent news story gives a clear example. In a tremendous act of courage and character, a high-school quarterback gave back the honor of securing his conference's career passing record. Why? Because he found out how he got the record. Nate Haasis, a seventeen-year-old senior at Southeast High School in Springfield, Illinois, completed a thirty-seven-yard pass in the last game of his high-school career, giving him the career passing record for his conference. After the game, however, he found out that a deal had been struck to make the pass possible. With less than a minute left in the game, Haasis's coach, Neal Taylor, called a time-out, walked onto the field, and huddled with the opposing coach to strike a deal. Taylor agreed to allow the opposing team to get an uncontested score if, in exchange, Haasis would be given room to make his record-breaking pass.

When Haasis learned the truth, he asked to have his claim to the record omitted from the conference books. He laid aside the opportunity to be a record holder in order to maintain his character and integrity.[1]

We all face opportunities to better ourselves at the expense of truth.

It takes real courage to take responsibility, stand for the truth, and do the right thing. Here's what the Bible says:

- 2 Chronicles 19:11: "Take courage as you fulfill your duties, and may the LORD be with those who do what is right."
- Proverbs 28:6: "It is better to be poor and honest, than rich and crooked."
- Proverbs 28:13: "People who cover over their sins will not prosper. But if they confess and forsake them, they will receive mercy."
- Proverbs 28:18: "The honest will be rescued from harm, but those who are crooked will be destroyed."
- 1 Peter 4:19: "So if you are suffering according to God's will, keep on doing what is right, and trust yourself to the God who made you, for he will never fail you."
- 1 Peter 5:6: "So humble yourselves under the mighty power of God, and in his good time he will honor you."

Finding Your Strength in Him

In the final analysis, we must remember whom we are trying to please. Our courage can wane if we are simply trying to please people or protect ourselves. But when we realize that our ultimate reward comes from God, we can find our strength in him. We can confidently ask God for the help and courage we need to follow him.

Second Chronicles 14 provides a story of a mighty king who depended on God for his strength and courage. Asa was a good king who did what was right in the sight of the Lord his God. And because he was faithful to God and encouraged the people of Judah to seek God, the nation enjoyed peace for many years.

But even when we do what is right, we may still face battles; and such was the case for King Asa. An Ethiopian named Zerah attacked

Judah with an army of one million men. As they advanced, Asa deployed his own, much smaller army for battle. But Asa chose not to depend on his own strength or the strength of his army; he looked to the Lord. Listen to his prayer: "Then Asa cried out to the LORD his God. 'O LORD, no one but you can help the powerless against the mighty! Help us, O LORD our God, for we trust in you alone. It is in your name that we have come against this vast horde. O LORD, you are our God; do not let mere men prevail against you!'"

And guess what? With the Lord's help, Asa's army defeated the Ethiopians. The enemy fled, and Judah got the plunder!

As teenagers, we, too, will face battles, challenges, and temptations—especially when we are doing what is right. We have a choice: will we look to our own strength or to God's? The strength to be courageous comes from the Lord! As we choose to take a stand against sin and wrong, let's seek God. Let's ask him for courage to be the positive teens he wants us to be. After all, the courage we need to stand comes from him alone.

POWER POINT

Read: Daniel 1:8–20. What convictions did Daniel and his friends have? How did they show courage? (For more understanding about Daniel's courage, check out Daniel 6.)

Pray: I praise you, Father, for your wonderful presence in my life. Thank you for the courage and strength that you give me to do what is right. Thank you for your Word, which teaches me the right way to live. Help me to be wise in my behavior and courageous in my resolve to stand up for my convictions. Show me how to handle each situation with wisdom, discretion, and kindness. Most importantly, allow me to bring glory to you by living a life that honors you. In Jesus's name I pray, amen.

♀ **Remember:** 2 Chronicles 19:11: "Take courage as you fulfill your duties, and may the LORD be with those who do what is right."

☺ **Do:** Create a "Courageous Convictions" list. Take some time to think about the convictions you have based upon your faith in Christ and belief in his Word. Make a list of issues on which you feel convicted to take a stand (for example, alcohol use, premarital sex, cheating). Back up each stand with Scripture. Share your list with a friend, and commit yourselves to helping one another stay accountable. Ask God to give you courage when you face challenges and temptations in these areas.

Stepping Out
Moving past Your Fears

*This is the art of courage: to see things as they are and still believe
that the victory lies not with those who avoid the bad, but those
who taste, in living awareness, every drop of the good.*

—Victoria Lincoln

How many of your friends can say that they have ridden a bicycle across America? Our friend Billy Steadman has actually done it! At age sixteen, Billy rolled forward on one of the most exciting and courageous journeys of his young life. Here's what he has to say about his ride of a lifetime:

> When I first began thinking about a cross-country bike ride, I was going to do a five-hundred-mile ride in Canada with my grandfather, Bob Kiser, in the summer of 2002. But my grandmother got cancer, and we had to cancel the trip. That same summer, I went up to the Wandering Wheels headquarters in Indiana, because we happened to be close by for a family reunion. That's when I decided to go on their coast-to-coast tour.
>
> I wanted to do it because I had grown up with the stories of my mom riding from coast to coast in 1975 and the three crossings my grandfather had done. I also had heard all the stories of my grandfather's tours in countries all over the world, including New Zealand and China. My main fear about this trip was that it was

going to be very hard physically. Before the trip I was worried about getting in an accident that would prevent me from going. Then, a few weeks before I was supposed to go, I found out that I might have chronic mononucleosis. It turned out that I didn't have mono, but it did give me a scare. Even though I was very sick for the last month before the trip, God healed me, and I was OK.

God showed me that he wanted me to go on this trip in many ways. For one, my grandfather paid for the trip, which really helped. I would not have been able to go without his financial assistance. Everything went great in preparation for the trip. I was able to find just the right bike and got all the apparel I needed. Also, I never had any trouble getting used to riding on a bike seat all day.

The trip started in Seattle, Washington, and ended in Rehoboth Beach, Delaware. We traveled through Washington, Idaho, and Montana. From there we went down through South Dakota and into Nebraska, where it was straight east to Delaware for the rest of the trip. The entire trip took us seven weeks, spanning from June 19 to August 8. We usually slept in churches and inns at night.

God was amazing on the trip. Day in and day out he was there with us, keeping us safe and helping us get through each day. He reminded us of his presence through all of the people we met. In many towns, churches would put on a potluck for us. One town even got up at 5:00 a.m. to set up a snack stop for us about twenty-five miles into our day. The Lord also helped us get through the tough climbs and bad weather. On our second day of riding, we had to climb Stephens Pass, a sixteen-mile climb up a 9 percent grade in 40-degree weather. And it was raining. I learned that God puts mountains in our way to test our strength and our perseverance. He puts valleys in our lives to show that he still cares for us and loves us. God does amazing things, and he has no limits!

I learned that I could actually pedal a bicycle across the United States of America! To this day I still find it hard to believe that I did this. I also found out that the buffet is a biker's best friend, because we consume so much food (I spent eight hundred dollars on food for the trip). I would love to ride cross-country again, because it was more fun than everything I have done for the last sixteen years combined. There is just something about pedaling a bicycle day in and day out! You get a sense of freedom and accomplishment when you are doing it.

The only problem was that when I came back from the trip, I was no longer used to all the stresses of normal life. I was used to getting up every day, eating breakfast, riding a bike, taking a shower, eating again, and sleeping. I only had to worry about one thing every day, and that was getting to my next bed. Normal life has its demands and requires a different sort of perseverance and diligence.

My encouragement to anyone who wants to try this kind of ride is to recognize that it is so much fun, but it is not a walk in the park. If it were easy, everyone would be doing it—but that's what makes it exciting! Doing something bigger than you ever dreamed takes courage, but it's worth it. To pedal your bicycle from coast to coast, in weather ranging from freezing cold to blisteringly hot, from sunrise to sunset, getting stronger all the way, is a life-changing accomplishment. Great opportunities like this are not always easy; but they are worth it, and you create a memory for life.[1]

Courage for Your Calling

What is God calling you to do? It may not be as strenuous as a bike ride across America. It may be as simple as going across the street to minister to a neighbor. It could be reaching out to some of the lonely kids at your school or going on a mission trip with your church. The point is, we all need to listen for God's direction and courageously follow his calling. Often we are called to step out into unknown territory, outside our comfort zone, and that's where courage comes into play. As God guides us, he will also provide what we need for the journey.

We can see this courage to follow God's call throughout the Bible: Abraham stepping out into a new land to form a new nation. Moses accepting God's call to lead the Israelites out of slavery and into the desert toward the Promised Land. Joshua taking up the leadership role after Moses in order to lead the Israelites across the Jordan. David stepping up to battle Goliath and then to lead the people of Israel as their greatest king. Solomon walking in God's direction and wisdom as he built the temple. Isaiah stepping out to speak God's truth to the people of Judah. Jonah preaching repentance to the people of Nineveh.

In the New Testament, we see the same kind of courage: The disciples faithfully following Jesus and sharing his story after the Resurrection. The early Christians stepping out in faith to live and share the gospel in spite of persecution. The apostle Paul courageously preaching about Jesus, despite frequent beatings, death threats, and imprisonment.

Sometimes people in the Bible were called to do things that were inconceivable to them. Think of Mary, who was visited by the angel Gabriel: "'Don't be frightened, Mary,' the angel told her, 'for God has decided to bless you!'" (Luke 1:30). God had a great plan for Mary's life; through her, the Savior of the world would come. Was she frightened? Yes. Did she need courage to walk down the path God had chosen for her? Yes. Her strength came from the Lord.

Any great accomplishment or achievement demands great courage. Risk is not always a bad thing. Certainly it would be lovely to stay in our own little comfort zones and never be stretched or challenged; but then, we would rarely accomplish anything of great worth. Besides, only as we move outside our comfort zones can we know without a doubt that our accomplishments are God's work and not our own.

William Carey once said, "Expect great things from God. Attempt great things for God."[2] It's easy to trust God in the safe places of our lives. The question is, are we willing and able to trust him in the unknown territory as well? Are we ready to believe that God can take our meager gifts and talents and do far more with them than we could ask or imagine?

Don't Hide Your Talents and Gifts

Jesus told a parable about loaned money that illustrates the importance of stepping out in faith and not holding on to or hiding our talents and abilities. The story, found in Matthew 25:14–30, begins with a man who is preparing to go on a trip. He gathers his servants to give them money to invest for him while he is gone. To one he gives five talents (a talent was a form of money in New Testament times); to another he gives two talents, and to another he gives one talent. After the man leaves, the servant with five talents goes and immediately invests them, gaining five more talents. Likewise, the servant with two talents invests and gains two more. But the servant with one talent goes off, digs a hole in the ground, and buries his money.

When the man returns after a long time away, he brings his servants before him to see what they did with what he gave them. When he sees that the first two servants did well by doubling their money, he says to each one, "Well done, good and faithful servant! You have been faithful with a few things; I will put you in charge of many things. Come and share your master's happiness!" (Matthew 25:21 NIV).

Then the servant with one talent approaches his master and says, "I knew that you are a hard man, harvesting where you have not sown and gathering where you have not scattered seed. So I was afraid and went out and hid your talent in the ground. See, here is what belongs to you" (vv. 24–25).

Did you notice that the third servant said, "I was afraid"? How stifling those words can be! They can keep us from stepping out in faith to accomplish all that God has planned for us. Here's how the master replied:

> You wicked, lazy servant! So you knew that I harvest where I have not sown and gather where I have not scattered seed? Well then, you should have put my money on deposit with the bankers, so that when I returned I would have received it back with interest. Take the talent from him and give it to the one who has the ten talents. For everyone who has will be given more, and he will have an abundance. Whoever does not have, even what he has will be taken from him. And throw that worthless servant outside, into the darkness, where there will be weeping and gnashing of teeth. (vv. 26–30)

Parables are stories that have deeper meanings than can be seen on the surface. This particular parable has to do with more than money; it has to do with our talents and gifts—everything that God has given us to help us make an impact on our world. Let's not end up like the servant who was too fearful to work with the gifts he had! To be positive teens, we must be faithful, not fearful. It doesn't matter how talented or gifted we think we are. Notice, the first servant in the parable was given more talents than the second servant, and the second servant was given more talents than the third. We may not have the same degree of talent or gifting as the next person. But all of us are required to be faithful and courageous with what we have been given.

Last year, I (Grace) was stretched in this area when I decided to work with an outreach ministry through my school. Our assignment was to go as a team of teenagers to low-income apartment complexes and build relationships with the kids there, sharing Christ's love through our actions and words. Although I was fearful at first and definitely out of my comfort zone, God gave me courage, and I was able to use my gifts and my love for the Lord in a fresh, bold way. Our team saw many lives begin to change through our simple acts of kindness and service.

Taking Risks and Changing Directions

Courage doesn't guarantee that we'll get the exact outcome we want. In fact, our courage may lead us to a new place, a different place than we thought it would take us. When we find ourselves in that new place, we need to continue to persevere and have the courage to move in a new direction. One of our closest friends, Lane, has learned what it means to be flexible and adjust to God's plan. We'll let her tell her own story:

> Being born with a complication in my leg caused many challenges when it came to participating in sports. I loved playing basketball and tried to play every day. My leg gave me problems occasionally during practice and games, but I kept playing. I was born with a vascular anomaly that would swell up and cause extreme pain. While running, my leg would even drag at times. When I was young, I was able to cope with the pain; however, when I was fourteen, I was unable to overcome the pain and swelling. I had great trouble running.
>
> After visiting my doctor, it was determined that I would need several surgeries. I was fearful of the possibilities but knew I needed to at least try the option of surgery, with no guarantee of the results. Although the surgeries reduced the pain, my leg was not completely healed. I began to realize and accept the fact that I may not be able to play basketball on the school team. So what did God have for me? I had a choice: to give up and feel sorry for myself, or face the unknown and think of some new and different ways to use my gifts and talents.

Be strong with the Lord's mighty power. —Ephesians 6:10

Although God did not intend for me to play basketball, he opened up the door for me to get involved in other extracurricular activities, such as kickboxing. Though this was not my first intention, I made the choice to follow where God was leading me; and in return, I developed new friendships as well as a lasting activity.[3]

Sometimes, like Lane, we need the courage to adjust. Maybe we didn't get elected to the student council or make the team or win the competition. Maybe we didn't get accepted to our first-choice college. Maybe the boyfriend or girlfriend we thought was "forever" wasn't. When things don't work out exactly as we had hoped, we must not give up. Instead, we must continue to look to God for direction, face our fear of the unknown, and step forward with courage to try a different route or a new idea.

David had to take a few new routes in his life when he was being chased by King Saul. At one point he wrote these words in Psalm 27:11–14:

Teach me how to live, O LORD.
> Lead me along the path of honesty,
> for my enemies are waiting for me to fall.
Do not let me fall into their hands.
> For they accuse me of things I've never done
> and breathe out violence against me.
Yet I am confident that I will see the LORD's goodness
> while I am here in the land of the living.
Wait patiently for the LORD.
> Be brave and courageous.
> Yes, wait patiently for the LORD.

Courage doesn't mean forging foolishly ahead. Rather, it means taking firm, careful, patient steps, as we are led and guided by God.

Following our own intentions may lead us to slippery rocks. But following God's plan will always lead us to solid ground. As we seek to become positive teens, may our prayer be like David's in Psalm 61:1–3 (NIV): "Hear my cry, O God; listen to my prayer. From the ends of the earth I call to you, I call as my heart grows faint; lead me to the rock that is higher than I. For you have been my refuge, a strong tower against the foe."

POWER POINT

Read: Nehemiah 1:1–11, 2:1–8, and 6:15–16. What great thing did Nehemiah want to do? How did he handle his fear of stepping out? What did God accomplish through Nehemiah's courage and faithfulness?

Pray: Mighty and powerful God, you can do all things. I praise you, for your plans are perfect. Thank you for giving me the courage to step out in faith and accomplish the tasks you set before me. I depend on you, Lord, to see me through. Keep my ears attentive to your calling and my eyes open to your leading. Thank you for being my strength today and every day. In Jesus's name I pray, amen.

Remember: Psalm 31:24: "So be strong and take courage, all you who put your hope in the LORD!"

Do: Is there anything that you sense God is calling you to do in your life, yet you are fearful of stepping forward? Stop and ask God right now to give you the courage to carry out what he is telling you to do. Do all you can to plan and prepare wisely, and leave the fear to him. Write down what you plan to do and when you will do it. You may want to share the plan with a friend, so he or she can give you encouragement and hold you accountable.

Conclusion

Reaching Forward
Planning for a Positive Future

*If you keep yourself pure, you will be a utensil
God can use for his purpose.
Your life will be clean, and you will be ready for
the Master to use you for every good work.*

—2 Timothy 2:21

Imagine packing your bags, getting into the car, and heading off for spring break with your family. As you sit in the backseat ready to plug in your favorite CD, you ask your dad, "So where are we headed?"

"I'm not quite sure," he casually replies. "I guess we'll know when we get there."

Now you may be thinking to yourself, *That's ridiculous. No family does that. When a family takes a vacation, they usually have at least an idea of where they are going!* True. But many people do something even nuttier: they head off on their journey down the road of life, letting the road lead them wherever it goes. Their bags are packed, but they have no plan, no purpose; they just go with the flow.

We hope that after reading this book, your bags are packed and you are ready to journey down the road of your life. Our goal has been to equip you with seven powerful principles to help your journey be a positive one. We have encouraged you to take with you:

- A confidence in who God made you to be
- Tips on being responsible in work and in life
- The desire to live and speak with integrity

- An ability to develop and deepen important relationships
- An attitude of hope and joy
- A sincere and vibrant faith in God
- The courage to face your fears and stand up for your convictions

With these assets packed into your character, you are sure to go far in life. But what's your destination? Unlike the foolish family on their trip to Nowhere, we can know where our final destination is. We may have some unexpected twists and turns along the way, and we may not know exactly what's on the road just ahead; but we can be sure that we're headed to a wonderful place. Ultimately, as Christians, we will end up in our heavenly home with our loving Father God, who will say the words we long to hear: "Well done, my good and faithful servant!"

Are We There Yet?

Perspective is everything. When we stand outside a tall building or a large mall, the structure seems enormous from our perspective. But if we look at that same building from an airplane high in the sky, it seems like a miniature. The same is true of life. From where we are standing in life right now, some issues may seem really big to us. But when we take a look at our lives in light of eternity, those same issues may not look so overwhelming.

We're not saying that certain big issues in our lives aren't important. What we *are* saying is that an eternal perspective can help us see things a little more clearly in the present.

Throughout the pages of his best-selling book, *The Purpose-Driven Life*, Rick Warren continually reminds us of the eternal picture. He keeps us focused on the fact that life on earth is temporary and that we are preparing for heaven. "We never really own anything during our brief stay on earth," Warren says. "God just loans the earth to us while we're here. It was God's property before you arrived, and God will loan it to someone else after you die. You just get to enjoy it for a while."[1]

When we realize that this life isn't all there is, we can look toward the future with hope and confidence. Isn't it wonderful to know we are headed for a good place? The road we travel here on earth may not always be smooth. In fact, we're sure to have some bumps, detours, and U-turns along the way. But just as with any road trip, the destination is what's important. That's what we look forward to.

Think about it. Probably every single one of us is guilty of having relentlessly badgered our parents with, "How much longer until we get there?" or, "Are we there yet?" Why do we whine during the trip? Because we know that where we are going is so much better than where we are, cramped up in the backseat with our siblings! We can try to make the best of being in the car, but we're really looking forward to reaching our destination.

What's in Your Future?

In his book *The Present*, Dr. Spencer Johnson tells the story of a young man who discovers one of the greatest secrets to being happy and successful at work and in life. In a nutshell, it comes down to three key points: *be* in the present, *learn* from the past, and *plan* for the future.[2] What a great philosophy for us all! Although Dr. Johnson was talking about planning for our future here on earth, we can add our own "heavenly twist" and plan for our eternal future too.

As Jesus prepared to go to the cross, he talked to his disciples about the present and the future. Here's what he said in John 14:1–7:

> "Don't be troubled. You trust God, now trust in me. There are many rooms in my Father's home, and I am going to prepare a place for you. If this were not so, I would tell you plainly. When

everything is ready, I will come and get you, so that you will always be with me where I am. And you know where I am going and how to get there."

"No, we don't know, Lord," Thomas said. "We haven't any idea where you are going, so how can we know the way?"

Jesus told him, "I am the way, the truth, and the life. No one can come to the Father except through me. If you had known who I am, then you would have known who my Father is. From now on you know him and have seen him!"

Jesus, recognizing that he was about to be crucified, encouraged his disciples to have an eternal perspective. We ought to have an eternal perspective as well. We need to believe that God has a plan and a purpose for each of our lives and that we can look to him for guidance, strength, and direction as his plan unfolds.

We have a high calling and an eternal purpose as Christians. Yes, we're just teenagers, and we don't know all the details of our future here on earth. But we can know our purpose. When Jesus was asked to reveal the most important commandment, he replied, "You must love the Lord your God with all your heart, all your soul, and all your mind" (Matthew 22:37). As positive teens, our main purpose and passion ought to be to love, honor, and glorify God—which is a much greater purpose than simply living to honor and please ourselves. Ephesians 1:12 says, "God's purpose was that we who were the first to trust in Christ should praise our glorious God." As we live to bring glory to God, our life has meaning. We can trust him with the plans for our life, knowing that he loves us.

Making a Positive Impact

While we're on the journey of life, with our eyes on our heavenly home, we have a choice: will we make a positive impact on the lives around us, or will we be a negative influence? After reading this book, our hope is that your deepest desire is to make a positive difference in your world. Whether your time on earth is short or long, difficult or easy, you can still leave a positive mark.

Emily Hunter of Arlington, Texas, was a tremendous example of a positive teen. She had a 4.0 grade point average and was a member of the Lady Colts soccer team, the Key Club, and the National Honor Society. She was even crowned the 2003 homecoming queen—despite the fact that two years earlier, she had been diagnosed with an aggressive form of cancer. During those two years, she underwent twenty surgeries, including the amputation of her right arm. Amazingly, Emily returned to the soccer field just a few months after the amputation. She was ever resilient, determined, and positive.

Emily's one great wish was to get her high-school diploma. "Even when her counts were very low, she would drag herself to school," her mother said. "She wanted to be around her friends. She wanted to be in her classes to hear her teachers teach. She amazed me."

"She gave 110 percent and then wanted to know what else she could do," her English teacher recounted. "She was so strong and positive. She remained focused on living life to the fullest. . . . She taught us to live life to the fullest."

When the school learned of Emily's graduation wish, they tallied her credits and let her mother know that she had earned enough to graduate. But the day before her specially planned graduation, Emily died at her home, surrounded by her family.

Still, Emily's giving didn't stop. As she had requested, her body was donated to the University of Texas Southwestern Medical Center in Dallas, in hopes that it might help someone else.

As sad as her premature death was, Emily's life was an encouragement to all who knew her.

I am still not all I should be, but I am focusing all my energies on this one thing: forgetting the past and looking forward to what lies ahead. —Philippians 3:13

"She's been such an inspiration to all of us," her high-school guidance counselor said. "She fought a hard battle, but always with her chin up."

"She was an awesome kid," another teacher added. "I never saw her frown. Even when I knew she wasn't doing well, I asked her how she was doing, and her reply was, 'I'm doing as well as anyone.'"

Emily chose to be positive until her dying day. Although her journey was short and very difficult, she chose to make the best of her time on earth. Her life, characterized by a positive spirit, influenced hundreds of people who will never forget her.[3]

What can we learn from Emily's experience? That no matter how short or long the journey, no matter how rough or easy the road, we can choose to make life on earth a positive trip. When we plan for the future by choosing to place our lives in God's powerful hands, we can have a lasting and positive influence in this world.

By keeping our eyes on our destination of heaven, the purpose of our journey on earth seems clearer: to honor and glorify God in all that we do. What has God given you to do? Whatever it is, do it to honor him! Choose to live victoriously and joyfully here on earth, knowing that God is with you, and he will be with you every step of the way. Even now he is preparing an ultimate destination that is more wonderful than you could ever imagine. So go ahead, choose to become a positive teen. That's God's plan—and our prayer—for *you*.

POWER POINT

Read: Micah 6:6–8. What instructions for life are found in this passage? Next, read John 3:16–17. What do we need to do to plan for our eternal future?

Pray: Awesome God and glorious Father, how wonderful to know that you have great plans for my life, both here on earth and in heaven! Thank you for preparing a place for me. Thank you for sending your

Son, Jesus, to pay the penalty for my sin and provide the way for me to spend eternity with you. I want to follow you all the days of my life. May my life be a positive influence upon others, always pointing toward you. In Jesus's name I pray, amen.

♀ **Remember:** Proverbs 12:28: "The way of the godly leads to life; their path does not lead to death."

☺ **Do:** As you consider what you have learned in this book, finish the following thoughts:

- Some of the lessons I have learned from my past experiences include . . .
- I plan to live positively in the present by . . .
- I have planned for my eternal future by . . .

Notes

Chapter 1: Being Positively Who You Are

1. Croft M. Pentz, *The Complete Book of Zingers* (Wheaton, Ill.: Tyndale, 1990), 290.

2. Glenn Van Ekeren, ed., *Speaker's Sourcebook II* (Englewood Cliffs, N.J.: Prentice Hall, 1994), 26.

Chapter 3: Perfect Creation

1. Peggy Anderson, *Great Quotes from Great Women* (Lombard, Ill.: Celebrating Excellence Publishing, 1992), 11.

Chapter 4: Profound Purpose

1. J. C. Webster and K. Davis, ed., *A Celebration of Women* (Southlake, Tex.: Watercolor Books, 2001), 146.

2. Rick Warren, *The Purpose-Driven Life* (Grand Rapids: Zondervan, 2002), 17.

Chapter 5: Success 101

1. William J. Bennett, ed., *The Book of Virtues* (New York: Simon & Schuster, 1993), 355.

2. Van Ekeren, *Speaker's Sourcebook II*, 393.

3. Ibid., 392.

4. Bennett, *Book of Virtues*, 392.

5. Ibid., 364.

Chapter 6: Who Wants to Be a Millionaire?

1. Distributed at Dallas Bible Church by Pastor Hal Habecker (2003).

2. Edward K. Rowell, ed., *Quotes and Idea Starters for Preaching and*

Teaching (Grand Rapids: Baker, 2000), 114.

3. Van Ekeren, *Speaker's Sourcebook II*, 382.

4. John Rogers and Peter McWilliams, *Wealth 101* (Los Angeles: Mary Books/Prelude Press, 1992).

Chapter 7: Living It Out

1. Walter B. Knight, *Knight's Master Book of 4,000 Illustrations* (Grand Rapids: Eerdmans, 1956), 72.

2. *Webster's New World Dictionary* (New York: World Publishing, 1966), 759.

3. Rowell, *Quotes and Idea Starters*, 89.

4. Bennett, *Book of Virtues*, 608.

5. Ibid., 604.

6. Gerry Fraley, "Sports Day." *Dallas Morning News*, August 9, 2003, 1C.

Chapter 8: Reinventing Honesty

1. Michelle Malkin, "What's So Funny about Abstinence, Mr. Franken?" Distributed by Creators Syndicate and appearing in the *Dallas Morning News*, August 25, 2003.

2. Information provided by http://www.BlueSuitMom.com in *Trendsetter Report*, August 2003.

Chapter 9: Friends Forever

1. Louise Bachelder, ed., *On Friendship: A Selection* (White Plains, N.Y.: Peter Pauper Press, 1966), 5.

2. Norman Vincent Peale, *My Favorite Quotations* (New York: Harper Collins, 1990), 57.

3. Bachelder, *On Friendship*, 58.

4. John Cook, compiler, *The Book of Positive Quotes* (Minneapolis: Fairview Press), 96.

5. Bachelder, *On Friendship*, 57.

Chapter 10: Family Feud

1. "The Ten Traits of a Healthy Family" is used by permission from Dr. Jeff Warren, First Baptist Church, McKinney, Texas.

Chapter 11: The Dating Game

1. Justin Lookadoo and Hayley Morgan, *Dateable: Are You? Are They?* (Grand Rapids: Fleming H. Revell, 2003), 29.
2. Provided by Marilyn Morris, founder of Aim for Success, and used with permission. Check out the Aim for Success Web site at http://www.aim-forsuccess.org.

Chapter 12: Having Hope

1. This story was written by Jennifer and is used with her permission. To learn more, visit Jennifer's web site at http://www.threefeetdeep.net.

Chapter 13: Got Joy?

1. Roy B. Zuck, *The Speaker's Quote Book* (Grand Rapids: Kregel, 1997), 215.
2. Pentz, *Complete Book of Zingers.*

Chapter 15: A Spiritual Sensation

1. Knight, *Knight's Master Book,* 29–30.

Chapter 16: Standing Up

1. Jim Litke, "Haasis Shuns Easy Way Out," The Associated Press, November 8, 2003, at http://www.aolsvc.news.aol.com.

Chapter 17: Stepping Out

1. This story was told to us and used by permission from Billy Steadman, Frisco, Texas (November 2003).
2. Marcia Ford, *The Pocket Devotional for Teens* (Tulsa: Honor Books, 2002), 130.
3. Used with Lane's permission.

Conclusion: Reaching Forward

1. Warren, *Purpose-Driven Life,* 44.
2. Spencer Johnson, MD, *The Present* (New York: Doubleday, 2003), 81.
3. Toya Lyn Stewart, "One Day Shy of Graduation," *Dallas Morning News*, November 12, 2003, 1B.

CPSIA information can be obtained at www.ICGtesting.com
Printed in the USA
LVOW13s2224240314

378756LV00001B/242/P